CONRAD AND
THE HUMAN DILEMMA

CONRAD AND
THE HUMAN DILEMMA

By

CHRISTOPHER
COOPER

1970
CHATTO & WINDUS
LONDON

Published by
Chatto & Windus Ltd
40 William IV Street
London WC2

*

Clarke, Irwin & Co. Ltd
Toronto

SBN 7011 1587 4

PR6005
.O46Z662

Printed in Great Britain by
Butler & Tanner Ltd, Frome and London

CONTENTS

5

267083

Preface

MUCH Conrad criticism has been recently concerned with the autobiographical implications of the novels. This aspect is however not nearly so important as the overall guiding principles which Conrad indicates in his finest writing. This study does not set out to prove the personal importance of these principles to Conrad, but rather concerns itself with the technique Conrad uses for ensuring that his readers will come to those moral conclusions demanded by his artistic purpose in writing fiction. The chief interest here is the way in which Conrad suggests in a novel an overall morality often quite different from the morality of any character contained in the novel. Thus I have here attempted to examine the different moralities of all the major protagonists, to set these moralities against the overall morality of the book, and so to allow an increased awareness of what conduct is to be approved, and what not.

Clearly, it would be little short of a marathon task to do this for all Conrad's major fiction, and so this study limits its concern to the three main political novels, *The Secret Agent, Under Western Eyes* and *Nostromo*. These have, at least superficially, a theme in common.

Initially I have made some attempt to analyse and set down those critical assumptions I bring to my own reading of Conrad, and to bear these in mind throughout my discussion. But the real interest of this study lies in what Conrad has to say about character and conduct—that is in the moral foci of the novels—and also the way in which he says it. In all three novels, the morality of the principal character is not the overall morality of the book, for Conrad, by different techniques, provides his reader with a stable morality for the whole microcosmos of the individual work of art, against which he can measure the moralities of the characters. In *The Secret Agent* much of the overall moral outlook derives from an idiot boy and from the ironic tone of the narrative. In the other two novels, he uses the delayed narrative tech-

7

nique to provide the norm and allows his characters to react about this. In cosmic terms, this central morality can be seen to represent an absolute morality.

Finally, by contrasting a character's morality with the overall morality of the book, and relating it to the success or failure—in both physical and spiritual terms—of the character at the end of the book, we may draw some conclusions as to what type of conduct Conrad can approve, for it should not be assumed that the overall morality is necessarily a desirable one. In none of these three novels does Conrad suggest it is, but he does at least suggest methods of survival within the public moral schemata he describes. Since however the environments of the three novels are so very different, no abstract conclusions as to Conrad's view on morality in general will be able to be drawn. Each work of art contains a fictional world of its own, and, while it may say specific things about our own real world, it is not a relevant exercise to use the morality of one novel to tell us about that of another, even by the same author.

It would be churlish of me to let slip this opportunity of acknowledging those who in their various ways have assisted this study as a whole; the University of Keele, which accepted some of the material which follows as a thesis for the degree of Master of Arts; and especially my close friend, Dr Andor Gomme, who sacrificed many hours to discussion and to reading the typescript and suggesting improvement; the Headmaster and Governors of Latymer Upper School, who contributed much assistance of various kinds; and finally my most ardent critic, my wife. I am also grateful to Messrs J. M. Dent, and the Trustees of the Joseph Conrad Estate, for permission to quote from Conrad's writings.

I

Introduction

I SUPPOSE one's aim, when writing an introduction to any study which attempts literary criticism, is to bring out one's own critical assumptions, and to give the reader some indication of what one is trying to do in the arguments which follow. It is with these two questions alone that I shall be concerned in my introduction.

(i)

Reference to the short bibliography which concludes this work will give some indication of that tendency in recent works on Conrad which I mentioned at the beginning of my preface, a tendency to concentrate on the autobiographical element in the writing. As I hope to show in what follows, this seems to me to be subjecting Conrad's work to ridiculously severe limitations. Like any artist, Conrad could only use his own experience to provide him with the material from which to create his novels, and Conrad was indeed fortunate in the wealth of experience he enjoyed in the earlier years of his life. But it is not proper, simply because a writer uses incidents from his own life, to assume that he is only interested in how life has treated him, and how he has reacted to this treatment. Conrad uses incidents from his own life to illustrate the environment in which the characters he creates can perform and react, and he then allows us to use these same characters to bring a meaning not just to the fictional existence within the framework of the novel, but to life as it exists for us in our own 'real' world. Dorothy Van Ghent was perhaps hinting at this relationship between the fictional and real world when at the opening of her study of the English novel she defines the novel itself in these words:

9

The subject matter of novels is human relationships in which are shown the direction of men's souls.[1]

Conrad himself was fully aware of the implications of the relationship between reality and fiction. The latter ministers to the former. Commenting on his own work, he has written, in the Preface to *The Nigger of the 'Narcissus'*,

> Art itself may be defined as a single-minded attempt to render the highest kind of justice to the visible universe by bringing to light the truth, manifold and one, underlying its every aspect. It is an attempt to find in its forms, in its colours, in its light, in its shadows, in the aspects of matter and in the facts of life what of each is fundamental, what is enduring and essential—their one illuminating and convincing quality—the very truth of their existence. The artist, then, like the thinker or the scientist, seeks the truth, and makes his appeal (p. vii).[2]

Conrad is seeking out systems of existence, as it were. He is using the fictional world to portray basic truths about the real world. But this does not mean that his purpose is necessarily a didactic one. Writing in the Author's Note to *Chance*, he mentions

> this art which, in these days, is no longer justified by the assumption, somewhere and somehow, of a didactic purpose.
> I do not mean to hint that anybody had ever done me the injury (I don't mean insult, I mean injury) of charging a single one of my pages with didactic purpose (p. ix).

Conrad's work almost suppresses the didacticism, and yet it indicates and teaches simply because of the close relationship between fiction and reality which it embodies. How this is done is not really my concern in these pages. Others have written at length on the symbolism in Conrad's work, as well as on its autobiographical quality. Indeed, few critics seem to go beyond these two aspects. In fairness, of course, one must acknowledge that in combination Conrad's use of symbolism and autobiographical elements is bound to result in a

[1] Dorothy Van Ghent, *The English Novel: Form and Function* (New York, 1953).
[2] All page references are to the Collected Edition of the works of Joseph Conrad (J. M. Dent & Sons Ltd, London, 1946).

work of art very closely allied to the real world as we experience it, though this need not prevent us from bemoaning the limitations of such a critical outlook. This whole concept of synthesis is also reinforced by Conrad's fictional material. He is dealing, to all intents and purposes, with us.

> The History of men on this earth since the beginning of ages may be resumed in one phrase of infinite poignancy: They were born, they suffered, they died. . . . Yet it is a great tale! But in the infinitely minute stories about men and women it is my lot on earth to narrate I am not capable of such a detachment (Author's Note to *Chance*, p. viii).

And he is dealing with us as if from inside. The world of fiction has become a total symbol for the world of reality. This is the homeophoric quality of Conrad's symbolism (*v.* Ian Watt, 'Story and Idea in Conrad's *The Shadow Line*', in *Critical Quarterly*, II₂, Summer, 1960), and this is the device by which the relevance and immediacy of Conrad's writings for us gain their force.

Conrad's basic theme is morality. But like any other generalisation, this is only a beginning. Generally speaking, morality is the theme of nearly all of Conrad's fictional writing. But clearly for a survey of this length, we need some rather more specific common factor if we are not merely going to glance in passing at just about everything Conrad has written. The three novels I have chosen for this study are related in having in common the theme of politics to a greater or lesser extent. Of *Nostromo* and *The Secret Agent* no further justification of choice is surely necessary. They represent Conrad at the height of his achievement. *Under Western Eyes* may at first seem a strange bedfellow for these, for it has neither the scope nor the power of the other two. This one must acknowledge. None the less, by its material and organisation it invites comparison with the others, and has without a doubt very real merits of its own, as I hope to demonstrate in due course. Like the other two it portrays individuals, as representatives of mankind, in various relationships with Authority, that is with politicians or, by a very skilful manipulation of personal allegiance, even with anarchists. And this gives

Conrad immediate scope for interplay between the two separate moral schemes which many of his novels manifest and an understanding of which is absolutely essential if we are to comprehend fully the moral aspect of these three novels.

(ii)

G. H. Bantock, in his seminal paper 'The Two Moralities of Joseph Conrad' (*Essays in Criticism*, III₂, April 1953), demonstrates how Conrad, as an expatriate, was "outside the organised scheme of society", and was thus able to take a disinterested view of both the individual and the society in which he exists. There is first of all a public morality, that is, an expression of values from the individual towards his environment. This may be an acceptance of a political environment or of a duty in a given situation. The example given in the original paper suggests that, at its best, public morality is roughly equivalent to "the Western spirit of the British Merchant Service". It implies a transcendence of self which finds its own expression in a public code of honour and conduct, such as appears for example in Captain MacWhirr, or Captain Mitchell. There is also, however, the private morality of such a character as Donkin, whose social morality involves bettering himself at the expense of the whole life of the rest of the ship. Thus we are shown the possibility of conflict between these two moralities. It is this conflict, where it exists or, where it does not, the relationship of the two moralities that I have used as the starting point for this particular study.

One further question that we need to ask is about the nature and origins of morality in society. When a person acts in any way that is not quite neutral, we may say that he is acting either rightly or wrongly. This judgement will, however, depend not just on the behaviour of the individual whom we happen to be judging, but on our own point of view as well. In other words, when A says to B, "You have done wrong," these words may be telling us something about B's action. They are also definitely telling us that A morally disapproves of B's action, and this may well be indicative of A's attitudes in general. Since a novelist presents both A and

B to us he must take further steps to ensure that his readers are coming to the conclusions about both which the artistic purpose of his novel requires. Many novelists circumvent this difficulty by writing in the first person—a method which still leaves some room for the reader to misconstrue the moral orientation of the novel; but if the artist has real ability, we will be able to distinguish between the real morality and the stated one, simply because of the nature of the discrepancy between the speaker's values and our own. This is exactly what happens when Browning writes a dramatic monologue. Conrad, however, rarely writes directly in the first person, but since it is vital that the true morality in which he believes must be projected, he chooses the device known as the delayed narrative technique. The story is told in the first person by a character other than Conrad himself, and very often called Marlow.

Now although initially this gives us a positive moral focus, it also allows Conrad to bring to bear on the subject yet another dimension of morality. For whereas Conrad may be making a judgement on, let us say, Lord Jim, he does this by incidentally making a different judgement on his narrator, Marlow, or by allowing him only a very woolly moral sense at all. Marlow appears in none of the three novels discussed here, but traces of him can be seen in the fact that two of them make use of the delayed narrative technique. *Nostromo* has its occasional first-person narrator in Captain Mitchell, and *Under Western Eyes* its permanent narrator in the person of the Professor of Languages. But it should be noticed that neither of these possess the dominating influence of Marlow over the novels where he appears. Mitchell is only the narrator for short sections of *Nostromo*, and the Professor, although his narrative is continuous, so relies on Razumov's diary for the material of *Under Western Eyes*, that he disappears almost entirely from our awareness for whole sections of the book. In *The Secret Agent*, Conrad's manipulation of character is so brilliantly worked out that we can derive our moral conclusions without reference to any first-person narrative whatever. Here the private morality of the novel's characters, deriving as Bantock pointed out from "an awareness of the force and necessity of egoism", can be judged from outside the novel without the need for a narrator who is also a character in the novel. One of the things I hope to show when we come to discuss this particular novel is that Conrad forces moral awareness on to his readers by making insistent comparisons between the major characters and an idiot boy.

(iii)

As we know, the morality of a novel derives directly from the way in which the characters speak and behave. Speech and behaviour are themselves the two most useful clues any reader has when he comes to try to understand the characters in the novel. This is why here I have made my study one of character as related to moral orientation. Something more, however, needs to be said now about motivation as an aspect of morality. When we have a choice of action, particularly where, as is often so in Conrad, the situation is a peculiarly moral one, it is very difficult to know if what we think is right is actually going to be right. This is not quite going as far as the utilitarian moralists who justify moral rightness only by the outcome of an action. The point is that it is impossible to know absolutely the rightness of an action before that action has reached its conclusion. By and large one can make a pretty fair guess at it. But the accuracy of this guess will depend on both motive and morality in general. Conrad is always in favour of the simple morality but, out of fairness to us, he comments that, through no real faults of our own, morality on land is always much more complicated than morality at sea. In the opening pages of *Chance* he refers to the Shore Set, and the Sea Set, and, since these concepts are going to feature in later pages, we need to think a little about them now.

As I have already mentioned, private morality is equated in Conrad largely with the ego, while public seems to come from a sort of Merchant Navy Tradition. So Conrad allows his simplest form of morality to be that found on board ship.

The exacting life of the sea has this advantage over the life of the earth, that its claims are simple and cannot be evaded (p. 32).

We may deduce certain implications from this. Firstly that the simplicity of life afloat is not found on the land, and secondly that the claims of morality on the land may be subject to evasion. The impossibility of such an evasion at sea may be illustrated by a further quotation from *Chance*.

> "If we at sea . . . went about our work as people ashore high and low go about theirs we should never make a living. No-one would employ us. And moreover no ship navigated and sailed in the happy-go-lucky manner people conduct their business on shore would ever arrive in port (pp. 3–4).

At sea there is a necessity for following the moral code of behaviour for one's own survival. This necessity exists also on shore, but nowhere is it so easily apparent as on ship. All those who fail in Conrad, fail because of a weakness in moral vision. Similarly, by analogy, it is from the situation of being on board ship that those of us who comprise the Shore Set can gain help when we are faced with the problem of not knowing what we are morally justified in doing. No one can really help us with such a decision, since, as has already been noted, the motive may itself impart a certain morality to the action. We are entirely alone, as one is at sea.

> The solitude of the sea intensifies the thoughts and the fact of one's own experience which seems to lie at the very centre of the world, as the ship which carries one always remains the centre figure of the round horizon (*Chance*, p. 300).

This also implies that all moral problems, both those of the sea and those of the land, are essentially simple. Conrad writes of

> . . . my belief in the solidarity of all mankind in simple ideas and in sincere emotions (Author's Note to *Chance*, p. ix).

One of the things I hope to show in the chapters which follow is that what make the morality of the shore so difficult to unfathom are the surrounding issues and complexities which trammel up even the simplest problem.

(iv)

While still on the subject of morality, I should perhaps explain certain expressions used in this study whose meanings may at first appear to be ambiguous. A moral scheme or schema may have two applications. If we refer to the moral scheme of a character within the novel, we mean the point of view which that person adopts in his conduct, or by which he is guided when dealing with a particular situation. If a character believes that he is justified in taking a life for a life, he is following a moral scheme—a private moral scheme, that is—which is not the generally accepted moral scheme of today, at any rate for this country. In a novel, however, many characters may share this same moral scheme, but this does not mean to say that, even if every character in the novel does, it is necessarily the moral scheme of the novel as a whole. The novel itself may be advocating something entirely different. Although it can do this by the use of a narrator or by symbolism, its most likely way is by showing us what happens to people who act in this particular way. Since also this is a fictional world with which we are dealing, the results of such an action are irrefutable. It is irrelevant to a discussion of fiction to ask, if A had acted in another way, what would the outcome have been. If it had been important to the work of art to know this, the artist would have shown us, that is, always assuming that he has done his work well. Once we come to the world in which we live as human beings, however, the situation alters. All that we can really assume is that if we act in the way A acted, we may end up in the same situation as A. We may not, of course, but the fictional warning still stands, and even if it does not influence our behaviour directly, it can often give us the extra degree of moral insight into our own situations that we so much need. To a large extent this is really what reading is about, the exploration of our own personalities, the gaining of insight. In Conrad's writing this very often derives from the moral scheme not of any one character, or even group of characters, but from the moral scheme of the novel as a whole.

It is from consideration of the overall moral perspectives of

16

each of the three works of art that I hope to be able to suggest some conclusions about the importance of the issues with which Conrad is dealing, or of those values which he believes to be important. I do not think it is an unfair assumption if we say that a character who behaves in a moral way, and who is shown as being successful at the conclusion of the novel, is one of whose behaviour Conrad approves. Furthermore we may assess the approval of Conrad, or indeed of any other writer, for his characters by the measure of their success or failure so long as we are prepared to acknowledge that success may be measured as much in spiritual terms as in physical. We must not be deceived by material welfare. I hope by character analysis to be able to abstract from the person in the novel a moral scheme, relate it to the success or failure of that character at the end of the novel, and thus with a composite picture of all the characters, to arrive at a moral scheme for the novel as a whole. By only a slight extension of this, it should be possible for us to study what Conrad approves in conduct and what he condemns.

'The Secret Agent'

THE central character of *The Secret Agent* is, according to Conrad himself, Winnie Verloc, the wife of the agent, a woman whose whole life revolves around her devotion to her idiot brother Stevie. Verloc himself is a spy both for a foreign power and for the London police, selling information about a group of anarchists which meets at his Soho shop.

A change of personnel at the Embassy of the foreign power, however, forces Verloc into becoming an agent-provocateur. He therefore has a bomb manufactured in a varnish tin by the insidious Professor, but, in attempting to blow up the Greenwich Observatory, he only manages successfully to annihilate his brother-in-law. Obviously, the bomb outrage has considerable repercussions among the police, for once taken unawares; among the anarchists, who fear greatly for their comfort at home; and in the Soho shop. For Winnie, deprived of Stevie for whom she had made unproportional sacrifices, stabs and kills Verloc, is deserted by the one anarchist to whom she felt she could turn, Ossipon, and eventually commits suicide.

Even from a summary as brief as this, one can see that the novel divides into four different spheres of activity: the Police, the Foreign Embassy (which I shall call loosely the Political Sphere), Verloc's home, and finally the anarchical group which meets there. These spheres are unified within the framework of the novel as a whole by the figure of Verloc himself. The first section of this chapter will look briefly at this fourfold structure, and the major part of the chapter will then go on to consider the working out of moral values within these four spheres separately. And it will perhaps prevent unnecessary complications if I outline here the precise order in which I intend to discuss these spheres and their separate components. Sections ii and iii of the chapter will be concerned primarily with the Police, iv with the Anarchists in general terms, and v with Verloc, the secret agent, in particular. The rest of the chapter will largely deal with the domestic situation: Stevie in vi, his mother in vii, and Winnie in viii–x. The chapter will end with a discussion which it is hoped will bring all these together to provide the overall moral view propounded by the novel as a whole.

(i)

The Author's Note to *The Secret Agent* makes it abundantly clear that Conrad was acutely aware of the sort of criticism which the novel called forth. Non-literary figures like Lord Simon of Wythenshawe found in it "not one single noble act, hardly a really disinterested thought" (quoted in Mary Stocks: *Ernest Simon of Manchester*, Manchester, 1963, p. 46). But it is in fact this sordid climate which makes the novel so effective. For, as in the other novels here discussed, Conrad shows us different spheres of outlook, unified in this instance not by a theme, but by a person. It is this which enables him to examine the effects of a sort of amoral nobility in a particular domestic situation. For, as I hope to explain, Winnie Verloc is throughout motivated by a concern for her idiot brother which in its quality amounts to that nobility which stems from a desire to make life easier for others and operates to the complete exclusion of self-interest. Why in Winnie's case this is without morality is not really my concern at this early stage. It is only necessary to say that Winnie's concern for Stevie does not exclude self-interest so much as any publicly accepted code of morality.

Conrad is quite specific in showing Winnie as the central victim of the novel. Her centrality, which makes her also the centre of our interest, stems from her portrayal as essentially and rather pathetically the one truly human character in the novel apart from Stevie. Her centrality does not make her the unifying force. Verloc provides this. He is the one thread running right the way through the novel. He unites all the different circles of action. These latter can best be discussed under separate headings. In his capacity as secret agent, for example, he links the sphere of anarchy with that of politics.

Despite the similarity of their manœuvrings, Conrad demonstrates these two as opposing each other. Two further spheres, linked by the person of Verloc, and yet at the same time antithetical to each other, are the life which centres around Verloc's home, and the different activities of the police, which, not because I like the term, but because it provides a conveniently shorthand label, I shall call the Police Situation. As well as providing us with an opposite for the Brett Street shop, the Police Situation symbolises the complexities of official legalised (rather than legal) morality—that is, a public morality—since in itself it contains opposing interests. Heat and the Assistant Commissioner react and investigate in two different ways, and privately oppose each other while supporting the public fabric of morality.

It is because of these four subdivisions, Anarchy, Politics, Home and Police, and because of the fact that they are themselves often subdivided, that Conrad can show us rather more than four moral schemes of the type to which reference has already been made in the introduction. In this way, he can give us grounds for rejecting, or at least for examining, rather more motives. There is of course much more than this to the interplay of these divisions and subdivisions, for they are emblematic of the complexity which Conrad sees as the particular characteristic of the shore moralities, and gives him the stronger arguments for persuading us of the essential simplicity of what he sees as the only true moral orientation. However, before we can begin to understand the sort of moral behaviour Conrad approves of, his positives as it were, we must first examine the four spheres of action which have been previously listed. We must look within these spheres at what it is that makes characters act and behave in the ways they do, at their motives; and it is for reasons of simplicity and convenience, rather than of respective merit and importance, that I intend to deal first with the Police Situation.

(ii)

The Police Situation, as already stated, is an oversimplified and really rather unsatisfactory label for those sections of the novel where either Heat or the Assistant Commissioner or both are to be found. And it is worth acknowledging that to pigeon-hole them in this way is itself partly unsatisfactory. Despite the individuality of the separate spheres Conrad has integrated the novel as a whole so confidently that it will be impossible not to draw on the others while discussing the one. The Police Situation does not only overlap into the domestic one, or the anarchical, or the political; it provides a link unit between these last two, and itself contains situations which are themselves, at one and the same time, anarchical, domestic and political. Heat provides a link both into the anarchists' group—for Verloc is his informer—and also because of this, into Verloc's home life, his "domestic situation", if we need another label here. The Assistant Commissioner also approaches his work with motives that are domestic, and also political. Our labels, however, have already become too abstract, and therefore cumbersome, and so we must turn to the concrete forms of them in the pages of the novel itself.

Conrad places his police force in a consciously ironic frame-work. Within a single page of referring to

the true nature of the world, whose morality was artificial, corrupt, and blasphemous (p. 81),

he has shown us the police as

the great edifice of legal conceptions sheltering the atrocious injustice of society (p. 80).

The force of the adjective 'great' here, indeed its total connotation, and the source of the 'atrocious injustice' both of course refer to the 'legal conceptions' themselves. But this would not have become apparent without the judgement of two of the members of this same society, the Professor and Winnie; judgements which sandwich between them Conrad's own comments already cited above. Winnie's is the voice of distressed society,

"Don't you know what the police are for, Stevie? They are there so that them as have nothing shouldn't take anything away from them who have" (p. 173),

21

while the Professor is in a position to point out the self-consuming aspects of a society which orders and organises a police force for its own welfare.

> "Their character is built upon conventional morality. It leans on the social order. Mine stands free from anything artificial. They are bound in all sorts of conventions" (p. 68).

It is this last that most needs to be remembered in dealing with the two important police officers, Heat and the Assistant Commissioner. Beneath these two we have the splendid stolidness of the constable who exposes Stevie's remains to Heat in the morgue, and who had to use a shovel.

Heat naturally is, at one and the same time, afraid for his position, having just given assurances of peacefulness, and professionally curious, because his information had failed. This is not surprising since Conrad informs us that Verloc's secret agency has not been solely on behalf of the anonymous foreign power, but that he has been playing a triple game which has included the police in general, and Heat in particular. Thus Heat's position is of doubtful backing in a moral sense as well as one of personal security. His reasons for the race to Verloc which he has with the Assistant Commissioner are as personal and selfish as his rival's, but they stem from a sort of morality, a professional as well as a personal concern, and it is this professionalism which lies behind his attitude towards criminals, an attitude which itself stems from the very heart of this novel, that criminals have no difference from good citizens other than that merely of a different morality, nothing else. This, further, is set into sharper outline when we learn of the Assistant Commissioner's assessment of Heat to the Home Secretary:

> "He is an old departmental hand. They have their own morality" (p. 142).

Heat is, none the less, an excellent policeman throughout. His skill in detection, for example, as far as railway tickets and Stevie's name-tape are concerned, is impeccable. The author's admiration for him as a detective, however, is never allowed to cloud the true nature of his motives, for this is

what really matters. Although Chief Inspector Heat's knowledge of his subject is such that he can, very percipiently, say
to Mrs Verloc,

> "It strikes me that you know more of this bomb affair than even
> you yourself are aware of" (p. 207),

Conrad does not let us forget the selfish reasons for his race to
the shop, for

> He hoped Mr Verloc's talk would be of a nature to incriminate
> Michaelis. It was a conscientiously professional hope in the
> main, but not without its moral value (p. 202).

It is over the issue of Michaelis that Heat and his superior
become total antagonists. Both are on morally insecure
ground here, but Heat, possibly by virtue of his lower position and his previous method of gaining preferment by his
ill-acquired expertise at handling anarchists, is dealt with
the more severely by Conrad. While disgusted at his Chief's
unofficial conduct in personally interviewing Verloc, he has
himself behaved totally unofficially in his previous use of the
secret agent, and it is this, perhaps combined with his chagrin
at not having been first at the shop, that makes Heat "relieved
to see (Verloc) return alone" (p. 207).

The Assistant Commissioner's particular form of selfishness, while still providing him with motives which in an
absolute sense can only be described as immoral, is of a
totally different foundation from Heat's. Heat is comfortable
in his work, much, one suspects, as Verloc had been before
the opening of the novel. He is therefore concerned lest the
comfort of his position be shattered. The Assistant Commissioner suffers from moral discontent, not liking his job in the
first place, and having to use whist virtually as a drug. To
retain the last form of happiness in his life, which he can only
find at a friend of his wife's, he must protect Michaelis, whose
patroness this friend is. Hence moral schemata become thor-
oughly confusing unless we at once see the connection of
retaining domestic happiness by professional abuse, that is,
by the manipulation of one's official position. Hence comes
his attitude towards Michaelis,

"If the fellow is laid hold of again," he thought, "she will never forgive me" (p. 112),

and this compares strikingly with Heat's description of Michaelis,

"A man like that has no business to be at large, anyhow" (p. 113),

especially when one considers how splendidly ironical it is that both are motivated from essentially similar sentiments. Again in the discussion with Heat, the Assistant Commissioner extracts every piece of information he needs, despite Heat's unwillingness to expose his sources. He too is excellent at his job, despite his motives, and hence it is he who sees through the labyrinthine entanglements of Verloc's position right the way to the original instigator of the explosion.

"I've no doubt that Mr Vladimir has a very precise notion of the true importance of this affair" (p. 224).

In this way we find ourselves considering the political figures of the novel.

(iii)

Conrad's portrayal of Sir Ethelred is magnificent, and although he uses Toodles as an example of family manipulation into politics, and there is further an obvious irony in Conrad's choice of names for these two, he does not dismiss their political relationship as brusquely as this might suggest. Toodles is utterly devoted to the old man, and much of his conversation with the Assistant Commissioner shows his concern for Sir Ethelred's safety and well-being. The conversations with Sir Ethelred himself allow Conrad to include both lighter material and extensions to the ironic mode of the whole work. Hence one reads with delight the conversation about Sprats and Whales, and the splendid parallelism of a dogfish and the as yet unknown ambassador who is at the back of the Greenwich Park explosion.

We of course know almost from the beginning the extent to which Vladimir is involved in the whole business. His is the initial immorality from which the rest of the novel stems, for it is he who unscrupulously redeploys Verloc, the previously dreaded secret agent Δ of Baron Stott-Wartenheim, as an agent-provocateur for the political ends of his country. But he is made the more insidious for us by the two-sided nature of his personality. His visitor here is Verloc.

> For some thirty seconds longer Mr Vladimir studied in the mirror the fleshy profile, the gross bulk, of the man behind him. And at the same time he had the advantage of seeing his own face, clean-shaved and round, rosy about the gills, and with the thin, sensitive lips formed exactly for the utterance of those delicate witticisms which had made him such a favourite in the very highest society (p. 24),

—in fact in exactly the same society as that frequented by the Assistant Commissioner. One of the most interesting things about Vladimir is the tremendous difference between his appearance at this interview, and his appearance in society, and particularly on the occasion of his being interviewed formally by the Assistant Commissioner in the streets of London. For this disparity between appearance and professional character is exactly what he complains of in the person of Verloc, that Verloc's gross bulk, as well as the appalling fact that he is legally married, belies so much his role as an anarchist, a reactionary member of the starving proletariat. Vladimir's assessment of Verloc, his realisation of the agent's indolence, is of course right, just as he is right in not seeing the secret service fund as a philanthropic institution; and it is perhaps for this reason, and because he is only peripheral to the central drama of the novel, that Conrad provides us with no follow-up on Vladimir, beyond the fact that his role in the explosion is known to the Assistant Commissioner. That Vladimir was anxious to promote an outrage which would initiate proceedings against the London anarchists, that is, that he was primarily out for moral effect, can now be disclosed to the Authorities. For us, however, his having been right about Verloc is really only incidental. So is the fact that the Assistant Commissioner is right about Michaelis. Their rightness is unallied to the motives, in that their motives would have remained unaltered if they had been wrong. So in the case of Vladimir we can stand with Conrad in a form of condemnation which is made the more acute by the homily which Vladimir addresses to Verloc, and by our realisation that his is a world where art can count for nothing.

(iv)

The problem of art's place in society is, of course, never more than hinted at by Conrad in *The Secret Agent*. His concern is with the members of society and their behaviour rather than abstract activities which may or may not be of benefit to them. Hence the panoramic generalisations describing the environment in which the society of *The Secret Agent* exists. "Sordid surroundings" contributed with the alleged "moral squalor" to the dislike with which the novel was greeted. Conrad, in his Author's Note, explains his choice of London.

> There was room enough there to place any story, depth enough there for any passion, variety enough there for any setting, darkness enough to bury five million lives (p. xii).

This is the magnificently portrayed background to the above-world—it is not hidden enough to merit being called an underworld—of the novel. Conrad's treatment even of the physical environment continues utterly ironical, as for example in his references to London's 'strayed' houses alluded to during Verloc's journey to the Embassy, or when he (Conrad) says

> . . . the Italian restaurant is such a peculiarly British institution (p. 149).

But though the description of Brett Street, seen through the eyes of the Assistant Commissioner, is similarly telling, it is not with the surroundings that Conrad allows his ironic concern for general society to linger. Elsewhere, he comments on those who frequent the salon of Michaelis' patroness as

> Royal Highnesses, artists, men of science, young statesmen, and charlatans of all ages and conditions (p. 105).

26

It is within this total framework that Conrad focusses particularly on Verloc's "ostensible business", the incredibly shady
shop with its significantly cracked bell.

> ... this home, kept up on the wages of a secret industry eked out
> by the sale of more or less secret wares: the poor expedients
> devised by a mediocre mankind for preserving an imperfect
> society from the dangers of moral and physical corruption, both
> secret, too, of their kind (p. 258).

Here lies the central physical reality of the book, and, though
anarchists and anti-anarchists are to be found in salon as well
as shop, it is at the shop of the secret agent himself that the
anarchical meetings seem to be held.

The anarchists who come there make an interesting contrast with the anarchist who does not, the Professor; and it
is thus appropriate to this stage of the discussion that we now
turn to the anarchists themselves and later to Verloc.

Conrad's handling of the explosion in Greenwich Park is
in accordance with the narrative technique he uses so superbly
in *Nostromo*, and its full power can easily be overlooked on
re-reading, when one remembers the outline of the plot
chronologically. We gain our information at exactly the
crucial moment to enable us to piece it together accurately
without any loss of interest or suspense. When, early in the
novel, we have news of a man blown up in Greenwich Park,
we have a double reaction. Conrad's use of the word 'man'
forces us automatically into assuming that it is Verloc who is
the victim, for, though we have already met Stevie, our
analysis of him is on purely mental and emotional grounds,
and so we think of him as a boy, though physically he is a
man. Similarly we are compelled by Conrad's previous treatment of the Vladimir–Verloc episode, immediately to jump
to the possible national and perhaps international consequences of the explosion. Will it have the effects Vladimir
wants? The first of these is soon dealt with, for as a reader's
thought, it is irrelevant to the concern with individuals which
Conrad shows in the novel. The morality of the attempted
explosion at the Observatory, and the attitudes of the anarchists themselves

"This business may affect our position very adversely in this country. Isn't that crime enough for you?" (p. 71)

contrasts splendidly with

"To break up the superstition of worship and legality should be our aim" (p. 73),

and we are left with the problem of interpreting the bomb incident within the moral framework of the novel. How much is it a crime? How much is it a crime against the anarchists? How much is a crime against the anarchists a real crime? And, once again, Conrad shows us by the later development of the novel that our very formulation of these questions is wrong, for an action or an event is no absolute crime while it is still an abstraction, but only in the way it affects human beings. In a sense, it is another statement of "the Sabbath was made for man, not man for the Sabbath" (Mark II, 27). Society with a capital 's' is a virtually meaningless concept. The concern of any human being should be for other human beings; hence, as we shall see, the anarchists should provide us with a positive moral outlook, but do not; Winnie comes nearer to it but ultimately fails, and the only character who really succeeds is Stevie. He is totally annihilated, except for his name, by the amoral motivation of the society in which he has been forced to exist.

When one says that it is the anarchists who should be totally motivated by a concern for others, and are not, one is not implying a criticism of Conrad. This is his point entirely in including Yundt's manifesto,

"I have always dreamed . . . of a band of men absolute in their resolve to discard all scruples in the choice of means, strong enough to give themselves frankly the name of destroyers, and free from the taint of that resigned pessimism which rots the world. No pity for anything on earth, including themselves, and death enlisted for good and all in the service of humanity—that's what I would have liked to see" (p. 42).

But this is a long remove from the anarchists themselves. Self is still too near the fore of their motives and hence

Conrad immediately follows this moral statement with a list of adjectives which accentuate not just the grossness and fatness of the anarchists but the total impossibility of their living up to the manifesto—comical; unintelligible; worn-out; impotent; senile; toothless—and the futility is further marked by Yundt and Michaelis quarrelling over their pessimism. Michaelis, although we learn later that he has, according to his patroness, "the temperament of a saint" (p. 109), exists

in a mental solitude more barren than a waterless desert (p. 45),

and consequently when, at the end of the novel, we hear a report that Michaelis' philosophy is of the strong devoting themselves to "the nursing of the weak" (p. 303) we can immediately place it where it belongs. His book, in which he declares this philosophy, is totally irrelevant, not only to his own life, but to facts which he knows to exist. His writings are the insincere scribblings of a man who is glad enough to be left alone by the police, writing such hypocrisy and living off carrots. None the less, as we shall see later in the discussion, he provides an important comment on the internal situation of the novel.

Ossipon really belongs more to the domestic situation in the novel, in that his role is more pertinent to Winnie Verloc than to the anarchists or to 'The Freedom of the Proletariat', the subsidy for which he is so terrified of losing. It is he who is so afraid of the anarchists falling into public disfavour after the bomb outrage, for like so many of the other male characters in the novel he is essentially lazy, and only really concerned with having enough money personally. So after the supposed unintentional suicide of Verloc, he is more interested in the future of Winnie and the shop, a fact that is easily seen, incidentally, by the Professor. Ossipon, after Winnie has almost literally thrown herself upon him, and before he realises the true circumstances of Verloc's death, seizes every opportunity to gain preferment. But he is, even in this instance, as hypocritical as the rest,

"A love like mine could not be concealed from a woman like you," he went on, trying to detach his mind from material considerations such as the business value of the shop, and the amount of money Mr Verloc might have left in the bank (p. 274).

Conrad's treatment of Ossipon, however, is not as kind as what has been written above might suggest. He, above the other anarchists, is the one we most see in juxtaposition to the Professor, in whose presence Ossipon

> suffered from a sense of moral and even physical insignificance (p. 62),

for the Professor comes nearest to being a true anarchist. He, unlike any of the others, is the ruthless searcher in whose presence the law steps to one side. But he is searching for a perfect detonator, not the alleviation of the starving masses. Towards people he is as inexorable as any tyrant or dictator.

> "The weak! The source of all evil on this earth! . . . I told him that I dreamt of a world like shambles, where the weak would be taken in hand for utter extermination" (p. 303).

Certainly the Professor himself is powerful, clutching the rubber bulb detonator in his pocket. But even the Professor's power is limited, though he himself realises this.

> "The manner of exploding is always the weak point with us" (p. 67);

his pocket detonator takes twenty seconds to operate. None the less, what puts the Professor on his own outside the circle of anarchists, is that he has this single purpose, that of finding a perfect detonator. He knows what he is after while the rest do not, and thus he is the only one who is not playing at being an anarchist. He does gain power, however, from the fact that his assessment of right and wrong is invariably correct. He understands motives too; but his analysis is limited. He sees that what evil there is in *The Secret Agent* comes as a result of weakness from those characters who are themselves weak. What he does not define are the types of weakness between Stevie, born weak into a hostile world, and Verloc, made weak by being in a position of his own choosing.

(v)

This naturally brings us to Verloc, and it will perhaps simplify matters if we look at him first merely in his political context, as a secret agent selling anarchical information, rather than as a husband or a brother-in-law, which is his domestic role. This is the

> Mr Verloc, who, by a mystic accord of *temperament* and *necessity*, had been set apart to be a secret agent all his life (p. 180 —my italics).

The necessity is of course easy to see. It is the same necessity of which we are all in a sense victims, that of furnishing ourselves with a livelihood. But it is temperament linked with this that has forced Verloc into becoming a secret agent, into the totally immoral position of making friends so that he can betray them. For Verloc's judgement on the laziness of the anarchists can be nothing more than an attempt to shrug off his own responsibility. His basic trouble then is one of temperament; it is, as Vladimir was so quick to notice, his indolence. As a political figure, he is, as Ossipon has pointed out with splendid irony, a man of no ideas, who was useful only in that he could elude the police. As well as the double irony here, Conrad increases the problems of Verloc's situation by forcing him into becoming an agent-provocateur. Thus he has actively to indulge in anarchy while being the secret agent of a foreign power and a police informer. It would be a wholly ridiculous understatement to suggest that this represents a confusion of morality. As a character, Verloc is amoral in that he is without moral or even immoral orientation or motivation. He needs merely to keep his job as a secret agent because he needs the income.

As we have realised from the beginning, however, Verloc's function is in fact a triple one. As well as having a "vocation as a protector of society" (p. 5), presumably as a secret agent, he is also a seller of shady wares. But we are also told, in the opening pages of the book, that he "cultivated his domestic virtues" (p. 5). Conrad is unremitting in his stressing of

Verloc's domestic role. It is the Assistant Commissioner who
points out,

> "From a certain point of view, we are here in the presence of a
> domestic drama" (p. 222).

Verloc's greatest mistake, in fact, is not to see the connection
in his own life between political and domestic activity. Hence,
before the real domestic issue begins, that is just after Stevie's
death, he can say

> "I have been mad for a month or more, but I am not mad now.
> It's all over. It shall all come out of my head, and hang the
> consequences" (pp. 208–9),

and this failure to connect, this duality of situation, is perhaps
what prompted Conrad to include the symbolism of Verloc's
journey west to the Embassy when the sun bathes everything
gold, except for Verloc himself, whose overcoat appears rusty.
He is corroded as a citizen, that is as a husband, as well as a
secret agent. Incidentally, it is of course wrong to see him as
these three separate entities of citizen, husband and secret
agent. His values remain the same in whatever sphere he is.
This is the reason for his double failure, the latter part of
which he again fails to see.

Verloc seems as assured in his domestic relationship with
Winnie as he does when he replies to Vladimir in the Embassy.
It is with this husband–wife relationship that we must begin
the discussion of Verloc's domestic situation.

> Mr Verloc loved his wife as a wife should be loved—that is,
> maritally, with the regard one has for one's chief possession. This
> head arranged for the night, those ample shoulders, had an
> aspect of familiar sacredness—the sacredness of domestic peace
> (p. 179).

It is this peace which means so much to Verloc, the comfort
of virtual indolence which is so brutally shattered by
Vladimir's threat. His position is impossible. He must either
lose his livelihood, arrange the bomb, or perform the bomb-
ing himself. It is a choice which is of course the direct result
of his having a double position, a foot with the anarchists
and a foot against them. It is exactly the same sort of dilemma

which we shall see confronting Razumov and Nostromo in the other two novels which concern us in this discussion. The apparent morality of his decision is in accordance with his indolence: it is the easiest way of preserving the status quo. And this is the key to our solving the problem of his real morality. He does not have one. He is not anti-anarchist by conviction. It is just that being a secret agent was for him an easy and lazy way of earning a comfortable living. This laziness is what underlies the whole of his relationship with Winnie. He has never made the effort to understand her, or her love for Stevie.

> Only he did not understand either the nature or the whole extent of that sentiment. And in this he was excusable, since it was impossible for him to understand it without ceasing to be himself (p. 233).

Consequently the intimacy of their marriage never really seems to get beyond expressions of mild concern, or an exchange of pleasantries. For example, on the two occasions when Verloc joins Winnie in the bedroom, she expresses concern for his state of health, firstly when he leans against a cold window, and secondly when he walks around in his socks. There is nothing wrong with this of course. But this is as far as the relationship goes. She never makes any greater gesture towards him. On his part, Verloc's reciprocation consists in his being on the point of telling everything to his wife. She has heard him in his sleep complain about 'those Embassy people' but neither of them knows what this means to the other. In the end he refrains from telling her because, once again, his indolence stops him. And Conrad focusses our attention not just on Verloc's indolence but on indolence as the characteristic of mankind when he tells us that it is "so often the secret of good nature" (p. 180). This is Verloc's temperament again, and so explains the moral problem in its entirety. His character is most accurately assessed by Winnie's mother, about whom more must be written later.

> In Winnie's mother's opinion Mr Verloc was a very nice gentle-man. From her Life's experience gathered in various 'business houses' the good woman had taken into her retirement an ideal

of gentlemanliness as exhibited by the patrons of private-saloon bars. Mr Verloc approached that ideal; he attained it, in fact (p. 7).

It must be the only ideal he does attain.

The pattern of Verloc's relationship with his imbecilic brother-in-law, Stevie, is not at all dissimilar from that which he has with his wife. What is much more interesting is that he is used as a moral control to actuate Stevie's self-restraint. Significantly, of course, Verloc is totally unaware of his being of

> the greatest moral efficiency—because Mr Verloc was *good*. His [Stevie's] mother and his sister had established that ethical fact on an unshakable foundation. They had established, erected, consecrated it behind Mr Verloc's back, for reasons that had nothing to do with abstract morality (p. 175).

Thus we are faced with the fact that this is the truth about Verloc's morality. It is a wraith used to keep an idiot boy in order, used initially for the protection of this boy, but, because it is a wraith, because it is actually amoral, it destroys the boy without leaving enough conscience to mourn him. At Stevie's death neither Winnie nor Verloc come out of themselves enough to lament for anything beyond their own losses. For although we are told that it had shaken Verloc "morally to pieces" (p. 230), his perturbation is purely selfish. He attaches no importance at all to the death of Stevie, the human being, the wholly loved brother of a devoted sister. The barrier between husband and wife here is caused by lack of understanding, an understanding which might have been effected had any previous effort been made to establish a real relationship between the two. So, while he makes his miserable attempt to explain it all to her, the gas in the parlour "purred like a contented cat" (p. 231) and underlines the latent discontent of the marriage.

Verloc had never reckoned with Winnie; he failed to see the link running through the different strands of her life, as of his own. Thus the overwhelming egoism of his appeals to her

"What would it have been if you had lost me?" (p. 234),

34

are guaranteed to fail, for, as well as being self-centred, they contain no indications of the awareness of his moral position. At the psychologically wrong moment he takes his wife into his confidence for the first time ever, and Stevie even "passes out of his mental sight for a time" (p. 239). Even when he remembers him, his statements show no sign of moral responsibility for the boy's death.

"If only that lad had not stupidly destroyed himself!" (p. 253).

Furthermore, he forces more and more responsibility onto his wife, insisting that "it was a pure accident" (p. 257). Conrad's comment on Verloc's attempt at explanation is as powerful in its irony as anything else in the book.

It was a benevolent intention, but Mr Verloc had the misfortune not to be in accord with his audience (p. 250).

Conrad shows us here the nature of Verloc's amorality, stemming as it does from total selfishness, from a complete failure to take other people into account. His closing remarks on Verloc help us to grasp this situation; he suffered from

one single amiable weakness: the idealistic belief in being loved for himself (p. 288).

Verloc is wrong-headed certainly; but he is also pathetic in his wrong-headedness. He has confided in Winnie at the very worst possible time to try to establish a bond between them, and has incidentally suggested to her the use of the knife. This sudden outpouring must have come from his feeling the need for assurance, however, and while I am not suggesting that the need is itself immoral, one cannot but notice that here it is totally selfish. He expects much of Winnie, where he has given nothing, and where he has taken away everything she had.

This man, hurt cruelly in his vanity, remained magnanimous in his conduct (p. 254).

The very wording here accentuates the fact that this is not Conrad's judgement, but Verloc's opinion of himself. So he dies, and his death is more than merely physical. Conrad treats it as a symbol for the moral death which was its prelude. In this way Conrad stresses for us the fact that amorality is utterly negative. It solves no problem; it answers nothing. If it arises out of sheer selfishness, it is no better than positive immorality.

(vi)

This brings us now right into the centre of the domestic drama. So we come to the character of Stevie, and of his mother. Stevie is probably the supreme example of a moral positive in Conrad's writings. It is he, the idiot, who is the only member of *The Secret Agent*'s society to have a complete worked-out morality.

> He prided himself on being a good brother. His morality, which was very complete, demanded that of him (p. 172).

As one would expect of a writer who complained bitterly of the confusions of the complicated moralities of shore people, Stevie's morality is very simple. It involves, as the above suggests, duty and allegiance to his sister, and significantly, it is entirely selfless. This does not mean that Conrad entirely endorses Stevie's view of the world. Indeed his death belies this, but it allows some constructive moral statements to be made. For Stevie's life is, as it were, concerned with giving, or at least with repayment. His outlook is of the simplest, his acceptance of moral statements entire and unquestioning, as is shown by the use, already remarked upon, which Winnie makes of Verloc as a moral curb on Stevie. This of course goes a long way towards explaining why, in the artistic terms of the novel itself, Stevie is an idiot. He is alone among the shore people.

None the less, he is far from being a pawn or a cipher. He has very real feelings despite their simplicity, and ones which arise from the simplest, most fundamental and therefore most satisfactory of all moral schemes. When we first meet Stevie, as early as Chapter I, we learn two things about him. That he is really all Winnie has to love, and that he also has compassion. And this ability for feeling pity for anything other than self—with one notable exception, a unique emotion in the book—becomes strongest at the time of his mother's removal from Brett Street and his relationship with the Cabbie and the horse.

> . . . the tenderness to all pain and all misery, the desire to make the horse happy and the cabman happy, had reached the point of a bizarre longing to take them to bed with him (p. 167).

His memory, it should be remembered, is entirely faithful as to sensations. It only lapses as far as facts are concerned.

> In the face of anything which affected directly or indirectly his morbid dread of pain, Stevie ended by turning vicious (p. 169).

The notion of bed epitomises, with an essential simplicity, comfort and happiness. Where he cannot produce these for others, he becomes seized with a viciousness which can only stem from utter frustration.

However, it would be quite wrong to suggest that Stevie has no factual memory at all. Despite its tenebrous nature, it provides an important link if we are to appreciate fully Stevie's moral function in the novel. During the course of the same journey, the cabman utters the words "Bad world for poor people" (p. 171), and this rings some bell of recognition of a past occurrence even in Stevie's memory. To us it at once recalls the anarchical meeting which had been conducted within Stevie's hearing, and as a result of which Winnie had to calm Stevie down. We are left with the unavoidable truth that Stevie is the only real anarchist present at that meeting. As far as his motives are concerned, he is a natural anarchist, a genuine and emotional one. So we have a positive moral statement here, where the conflicting moralities of society are brought into stark outline. On the ideal, or perhaps one had better call it the rhetorical level, as far as *The Secret Agent* is concerned, anarchy is for relieving the oppression of the poor. Stevie, from his 'natural' standpoint, thinks that the police are for this, and, although Winnie tells him "The police aren't for that" (p. 172), she is not entirely right, nor he entirely wrong. Winnie's bitter comment on the function of the police we know to be untrue, or at least wholly prejudiced, and we are of course left with the paradox that within Stevie's interpretation of society, anarchists and police should be working to the same end. Nor is this as trite and bizarre as it sounds on first hearing. The natural extension of the doctrine which Stevie symbolises is to a society whose total endeavour is towards the alleviation of its poor, its discontented, its downtrodden.

I do not propose, at this stage, to take this any further; rather to leave the possibilities of Stevie's outlook stemming from an unconscious and therefore innate social morality which is basically natural and absolute, and to take a step back to Stevie's particular condition. His outlook is a general one focussed on society at large, and it stems from his heart. Indeed, since Stevie is an idiot, there is barely anywhere else it could stem from. It is however important for us to realise that, despite this, it is not at all self-centred. Unlike Verloc, and as we shall see to some extent unlike Winnie, Stevie does concern himself with right and wrong. Hence we cannot lay against him the charge of amorality. But because of the simplicity of his morality, there is no room for doubt in his mind. Where there is suffering, there is wrong; and to this we can add its necessary converse, right is the alleviation of suffering. It does not seem to me to be relevant to question the completeness of this outlook. Right may involve more than this but, within the terms of the novel, and particularly within the terms of Stevie's outlook, the alleviation of suffering is fundamental to what is right.

(vii)

If Stevie's morality is directed towards society at large, that of his mother is, as one would expect, based on the family. She is also the character who most seems to carry the symbolism of the novel. There is, for a start, the fairly obvious comment on her removal cab which was like "the Cab of Death itself" (p. 170). But before this voluntary and self-inflicted death sentence, as it were, we have a forewarning of her being like a judge passing such a sentence, though we do not know thus early that it is to be upon herself. Conrad has shown us in the opening pages of the novel this woman wearing a "black wig under a white cap" (p. 6). The inversion from the black cap on the white wig should have told us this, and we are left with having to accept the strange fact of the dedicated woman being almost a kind of doom, or at least hinting from the first not just at murder—physical or emotional—but at capital punishment as well.

The mother's assessment of Mr Verloc has already been quoted (p. 33). This helps to symbolise the limited moral environment posed on her world by herself. But within the moral vortex at the centre of which stands Verloc, Winnie's mother has far more homely, far more natural, and therefore far more sound guiding principles, and it is these that cause the moral gulf between her daughter and herself. Tillyard has pointed out (v. 'The Secret Agent Reconsidered' in Essays in Criticism, XI, 1961) that Winnie fails to understand her mother's motives in leaving Brett Street, despite the fact that she is herself similarly motivated. This really is rather simplifying the issue since, though both are utterly devoted to Stevie, Winnie's passion is not without its selfishness, while her mother's is completely self-denying. She was, we learn,

> going away from her children as an act of devotion and as a move of deep policy (p. 162),

that is, so that

> Stevie's moral claim would be strengthened (p. 162).

Conrad's own comment helps us to interpret this aright;

> . . . she was heroic and unscrupulous and full of love for both her children (p. 161).

The writing here concerns itself minutely with the pain her self-denial caused her;

> But it was hard, hard, cruelly hard (p. 163),

and the total lack of understanding Winnie shows for her mother's dedication;

> "That poor boy will miss you something cruel. I wish you had thought a little of that mother."
> Not think of it! The heroic woman swallowed (p. 163).

39

Such is the gulf between them, and such is the indication Conrad gives us of Winnie's moral outlook. Winnie, as many before have appreciated, is Conrad's central concern. The events of the book concern her more deeply than anyone else. Of course this does not necessarily mean Conrad's whole-hearted approval of her. She is shown from the beginning as Stevie's devoted sister, though the strength of her devotion will be missed on a hasty reading of the book. None the less we already know from the discussion about her mother that the extent of Winnie's devotion to her brother is limited by a narrowness of vision, and this we shall have to consider rather more closely.

(viii)

In the opening chapter, Conrad tells us of Winnie's "unfathomable reserve", and a wary reader will treat this as an indication of something more deep-rooted in her personality, perhaps a capacity for passion. It is important to notice also that the irony of Conrad's tone diminishes considerably whenever he is dealing with Winnie. He prepares us for his concern with her in his Author's Note.

> At last the story of Winnie Verloc stood out complete from the days of her childhood to the end, unproportioned as yet, with everything still on the first plan, as it were; but ready now to be dealt with. It was a matter of about three days.
>
> *This* book is *that* story, reduced to manageable proportions, its whole course suggested and centred round the absurd cruelty of the Greenwich Park explosion. I had there a task I will not say arduous but of the most absorbing difficulty. But it had to be done. It was a necessity. The figures grouped around Mrs Verloc and related directly or indirectly to her tragic suspicion that "life doesn't stand much looking into," are the outcome of that very necessity. Personally I have never had any doubt of the reality of Mrs Verloc's story; but it had to be disengaged from its obscurity in that immense town, it had to be made credible, I don't mean so much as to her soul but as to her surroundings, not so much as to her psychology but as to her humanity (pp. xii and xiii).

40

He sympathises more with her than with anyone else, even, for example, when she censures her own mother for moving.

"What I am going to do to cheer up that boy for the first few days I'm sure I don't know. He'll be worrying himself from morning till night before he gets used to mother being away. And he's such a good boy. I couldn't do without him" (p. 179).

There are three things to notice here. Firstly, Winnie's very natural concern for Stevie's reaction; secondly, the consciously self-centred way in which the whole speech is worded—this is no selfless devotion—and finally, the assertion of her dependence on Stevie. This last is an important clue to our understanding Winnie's nature. Stevie has virtually become an emotional substitute for a real husband. Although the last two comments of the above speech were clearly put in to protect Stevie in Verloc's estimation, her dependence on him is also true. He is, after her mother's departure even more than before, all Winnie has left to love. She is forced back into her simple consolatory belief that things do not stand looking into. For it must be remembered that she was herself once in love, and broke off the engagement so that she could find someone capable of supporting Stevie as well as herself. He really is the sole focus of her love and attention and affection;

"You aren't ever hungry." . . . he was connected with what there was of the salt of passion in her tasteless life—the passion of indignation, of courage, of pity, and even of self-sacrifice (p. 174).

This is one of the most telling strokes of human insight in Conrad's writing, the psychological transference in Winnie's life from her previous young man through the period of self-sacrifice when she gave him up, on to Stevie himself, together with the fact that the lost happiness of that marriage has found a substitute in increasing that devotion to Stevie which brought it about in the first place. This is why Winnie clings to Stevie more than she ever would have done to her fiancé had he become her husband, and this also explains how the self-sacrifice of giving up her own desires for Stevie appears to us at times, though erroneously as I shall hope to show, a selfish desire of finding the substitute for gratifying her family instincts in devotion to Stevie. This is why in *The Secret Agent*, the selfless at times appears to have a selfish quality about it.

Naturally one does not expect this to make Winnie's devotion to Stevie any the less noble, but it is vital to see that this devotion has become the sole end and purpose of life for her. Thus we can expect, when Conrad tells us that nothing in Winnie's appearance "could lead one to suppose that she was capable of a passionate demonstration" (p. 38), that if she has this capacity it will be in connection with Stevie, and we see further her relative concerns with her husband and her brother when Verloc's concern over the cash-box fails to arouse her at all, yet the immediate suggestion of the rampager downstairs being Stevie forces her out of bed and downstairs at once.

It is when she tries to fuse the husband–brother link that Winnie's lack of foresight leads to a real family crisis. Conrad suggests that Verloc's adoption of Stevie is what she had been working towards from the start. But this lack of foresight, this total incuriosity towards motives and consequences, is already beginning to amount to a sort of amorality. In this particular instance, what Winnie of course cannot know is that the catalyst has not been her machinations, such as they are, but those of Vladimir. None the less, she is allowed some pleasure in seeing Verloc and Stevie going for walks together, like father and son, before, through her unwitting comment that "he'd go through fire" (p. 184) for Verloc, she prompts her husband to use Stevie in the planting of the bomb in Greenwich Park.

Against this we must balance the weight of her sacrifice in marrying Verloc for Stevie's sake. To appreciate this fully, we must consider Winnie's life before the opening of the novel, and her relationship, already briefly remarked upon, with the butcher's boy. Right from the beginning, Conrad stresses Winnie's youth, her neatness, and her possession of the sort of sexual desirability which would appeal to a character like Ossipon.

Winnie Verloc was a young woman with a full bust, in a tight bodice, and with broad hips. Her hair was very tidy (p. 5).

However, Conrad warns us that there is a great deal more to her personality than what is apparent merely on the surface. It is merely her own lack of inquisitiveness that makes us feel that there is a sort of superficiality about her, a feeling which is entirely unfounded.

> As a little girl she had often faced with blazing eyes the irascible licensed victualler in defence of her brother. Nothing now in Mrs Verloc's appearance could lead one to suppose that she was capable of a passionate demonstration (p. 38).

I have repeated this quotation because it not only insists that Winnie is capable of passion but because it also demonstrates early in the book her overriding obsession with Stevie. This is the reason for her refusal of the butcher's boy whom, Conrad clearly states, she was in love with. But Stevie claimed her allegiance. So we must never underestimate the force and the power of her self-denial. Conrad, in writing about Winnie's mother, says

> She had never really understood why Winnie had married Mr Verloc. It was very sensible of her, and evidently had turned out for the best, but her girl might have naturally hoped to find somebody of a more suitable age. There had been a steady young fellow, only son of a butcher in the next street, helping his father in business, with whom Winnie had been walking out with obvious gusto. He was dependent on his father, it was true; but the business was good, and his prospects excellent. He took her girl to the theatre on several evenings. Then just as she began to dread to hear of her engagement (for what could she have done with that big house alone, with Stevie on her hands), that romance came to an abrupt end, and Winnie went about looking very dull. But Mr Verloc, turning up providentially to occupy the first-floor front bedroom, there had been no more question of the young butcher. It was clearly providential (p. 40).

This is the plain narrative statement of Winnie's sacrifice, but as yet Conrad has not used it to add dimension to Winnie's character, or meaning to our understanding of her. Despite this apparent unconcern on Conrad's part for driving the point home, we must realise the importance of his

43

occasional reference to Winnie's young man, especially in her vision of the past.

> But this vision had a breath of a hot London summer in it, and for a central figure a young man wearing his Sunday best, with a straw hat on his dark head and a wooden pipe in his mouth. Affectionate and jolly, he was a fascinating companion for a voyage down the sparkling stream of life; only his boat was very small. There was room in it for a girl-partner at the oar, but no accommodation for passengers. He was allowed to drift away from the threshold of the Belgravian mansion while Winnie averted her tearful eyes. He was not a lodger. The lodger was Mr Verloc, indolent and keeping late hours, sleepily jocular of a morning from under his bed-clothes, but with gleams of infatuation in his heavy-lidded eyes, and always with some money in his pockets. There was no sparkle of any kind on the lazy stream of his life. It flowed through secret places. But his barque seemed a roomy craft and his taciturn magnanimity accepted as a matter of course the presence of passengers (p. 243).

This tells us how great Winnie's sacrifice has been in personal terms. The one bright aspect of her miserable existence she denied herself so that Stevie might not go wanting.

This is the only relationship of any depth which Winnie experiences before Stevie's death, or with any person other than Stevie. Even with her mother, Winnie seems unable to break through the emotional block caused by her overpowering devotion for her brother, to even a moderate understanding of motives. Indeed Conrad ties all her behaviour towards other people, relatives or anarchists, so that it becomes a continuous exemplification of her philosophy of life. Next then, it would seem best to examine Conrad's basic statement of Winnie's philosophy, and then to examine her behaviour towards those who make up the human element in her environment.

The initial statement in the Author's Note of Winnie's philosophy is one which is bound to colour our reading. But this does not mean that we should make a positive effort not to let it do so, for Conrad clearly wants it to influence us. He also refers to this statement at fairly regular intervals throughout the novel, and it appears further in the occasional phrase contained in many of the more important quotations which follow in this discussion of Winnie, in such expressions as "her wits, no longer disconnected" (p. 261) or "because she did not think at all" (p. 263). Otherwise Conrad's comments on Winnie's philosophy are not even loosely veiled. One recalls

> As not affecting the inwardness of things, which it was Mrs Verloc's principle to ignore . . . (p. 153)

and

> Winnie's philosophy consisted in not taking notice of the inside of facts (p. 154).

When first reading the novel, we know that Winnie's philosophy is a severe, possibly the severe, limitation in her personality, long before we discover the actual narrative form of the climax to *The Secret Agent*. It is the fundamental reason for her outlook, and the cause of her own personal tragedy. Furthermore, it can only be this lack of interest which has enabled Verloc to continue his agency without the interference of his wife. For although she is aware of the anarchists, her lack of inquisitiveness brings her separate stock reactions to the different members of the anarchical clique, but nothing more. She abhors Yundt, likes Michaelis and refrains from reference to Ossipon.

Apart from Winnie's so-called philosophy, if we are to understand her we must also be aware of her one motive in life. Conrad refers to it in plain statements and he also shows it colouring her every action. It is of course her devotion to Stevie, and whereas her lack of interest in people's motives is what creates the one half of Winnie's total personality traits—the negative part—the positive aspect which virtually reconstitutes her as a human being comes from her concern for Stevie's welfare. This is the sum total of Winnie in the cold terms of the clinical psychologist. What make *The Secret Agent* one of the greatest novels in the language are the mastery and brilliance of Conrad's translation of this psychologically simple analysis into all the complexities of a frustrated human being. Conrad is repetitively dogmatic in his insistence on Winnie's devotion to her brother. On page 195 he states quite categorically that "her only real concern was Stevie's welfare". Similarly, as early as Chapter III, after Stevie has been disturbed by the anarchists' talk, Verloc has to get Winnie for the simple reason that she is the only person who can manage Stevie. This is also another aspect of that isolation each character has from the other, and which culminates in the emotional exile of both at the time of the death of Verloc. This exile is in a sense the true consummation of their marriage, since, as we shall see, their whole relationship has been founded on emotional divorce. However, it is with this knowledge of the positive and negative sides of Winnie's personality that we can now begin to examine her appearances in the book right through to the brilliantly narrated murder scene and beyond, in rather more detail.

Now although one can in defining Winnie's lack of concern for personal motivation, easily dismiss it as amoral, one cannot get away from the fact that the book as a whole obviously proclaims a very definite morality. This clearly comes not just from Winnie's devotion to Stevie, but derives from the interplay of amorality and devotion which constitutes the amalgam of the total work of art.

Significantly, it is Winnie herself who plants in the mind of the dull and unwitting Verloc the use he could make of Stevie.

> "You could do anything with that boy, Adolph," Mrs Verloc said, with her best air of inflexible calmness. "He would go through fire for you. He——" (p. 184).

It is also her idea that Stevie should accompany Verloc on his walks. Everything is all right if it is for Stevie's good.

> "Could not get on without him!" repeated Mrs Verloc, slowly. "I couldn't get on without him if it were for his good! The idea!" (p. 188).

She is, as one would expect, unperturbed at the arrivals of the Assistant Commissioner, and later of Heat, but as soon as there is any mention of Stevie, Winnie registers "alarm and wonder" (p. 206). So Heat's analysis of Winnie also becomes right;

> "Mrs Verloc," he said, "it strikes me that you know more of this bomb affair than even you yourself are aware of" (p. 207).

This is the statement within the novel that comes nearest to the relationship between positive and negative traits in Winnie's personality. Her knowledge comes as a direct result of her love for Stevie, her lack of awareness from her minimal concern for the motives of others. It is also at this point that the novel begins to assume the proportions of the masterpiece it finally is. Up till now, we have tried to get to know Winnie, have failed, and have rejected her as something perhaps near sub-human. Now the passion of her existence begins to reveal itself, and we can accept her for what she is. Realising that Stevie is somehow implicated in all this business about a bomb in Greenwich Park, Winnie is desperately trying to overhear the conversation in the next room between Verloc and Heat.

> Mrs Verloc pressed her ear to the keyhole; her lips were blue, her hands cold as ice, and her pale face, in which the two eyes seemed like two black holes, felt to her as if it were enveloped in flames (pp. 209–10).

This is the first manifestation of passion that we see in Winnie, but it is no mere spark. It is part of the novel's overall irony that what creates this fantastic outburst in Winnie is not her limitation in terms of her character, but the positive side of her personality, her love for Stevie.

> Mrs Verloc sprang up suddenly from her crouching position, and stopping her ears, reeled to and fro between the counter and the shelves on the wall towards the chair. Her crazed eyes noted the sporting sheet left by the Chief Inspector, and as she knocked herself against the counter she snatched it up, fell into the chair, tore the optimistic, rosy sheet right across in trying to open it, then flung it on the floor (p. 210).

Beyond the plain narrative description of Mrs Verloc's passion here is Conrad's knowledge of the power of frustration within the individual, the collapse of a person's whole world, and Conrad symbolises that this is the end in the following words.

> ... the gold circlet of the wedding ring on Mrs Verloc's left hand glittered exceedingly with the untarnished glory of a piece from some splendid treasure of jewels, dropped in a dust-bin (p. 213).

For this is the outcome of the sacrifice Winnie has made in marrying Verloc. Conrad uses the ring as a specific symbol for this sacrifice, for, as has already been pointed out, sacrifice is, on Winnie's side at least, the whole basis of the marriage. But Stevie has been blown to little bits by the marriage partner, he is little more than refuse, having been scraped up with a shovel along with dirt and grit.

But this is of course only still creating the situation for the novel's real climax. It is in the next section that Conrad really demonstrates the extent of the individual exile of the two marriage partners here. One cannot pin any particular blame on either character for this. At least to do so would be considerably to reduce the power of *The Secret Agent*. Verloc does not comprehend anything beyond the negative aspect of Winnie's personality. In Conrad's own words

> he could not possibly comprehend the value of Stevie in the eyes of Mrs Verloc (p. 233).

But it is Winnie who has our sympathies right the way through, simply because of the nature of her devotion to Stevie and because she has sacrificed her own happiness that Stevie might be secure. So we see that any happiness she can possibly enjoy now must derive only from Stevie's security. The failure to understand this is yet another of Verloc's limitations. He is amazed by the passion of her outbursts and, true to form, treats it all with a rather indolent indulgence.

> "You might look at a fellow," he observed after waiting a while.
> As if forced through the hands covering Mrs Verloc's face the answer came, deadened, almost pitiful.
> "I don't want to look at you as long as I live" (p. 233).

Despite all this, the force of Verloc's conceit ("What would it have been if you had lost me?" (p. 234)) is such that he seems totally blind to the bitterness of his wife's despair. He sees her motivated only as he himself seems to be motivated, that is by conceit and self-interest. But Winnie is just the reverse. So Conrad's comment here is that the happy marriage of a Jack Spratt and his wife is about as true as generalisations usually are. Verloc has achieved his moral effect, but it is his rather than Vladimir's. Its success morally is on a personal rather than a political level. Furthermore, the superficiality of his own character makes it quite impossible for him to see what is the matter with Winnie, or even to understand her at all. ("What you want is a good cry." (p. 241).) And so that we can have no excuse for doing the same thing, Conrad, having given us during ten pages the exterior of Winnie's despair, as well as occasionally hinting at what is going on inside her, summarises the complete situation for us.

> With the rage and dismay of a betrayed woman, she reviewed the tenor of her life in visions concerned mostly with Stevie's difficult existence from its earliest days. It was a life of single purpose and of a noble unity of inspiration, like those rare lives that have left their mark on the thoughts and feelings of mankind. But the visions of Mrs Verloc lacked nobility and magnificence (pp. 241–2).

Winnie, to Conrad, is an heroic figure in the environment of London's squalor. This is why it is so important to remember Winnie's butcher's boy. Indeed, it is why Conrad refers to him at this stage in the narrative. For it is here that Conrad includes Winnie's vision of the past (v. p. 44). It is yet another factor to increase the size of Winnie's sacrifice. He had been the one bright spot in her miserable existence. But Conrad does not try to make Winnie's loss turn her into a new person, or give her a sudden new emotional life otherwise lacking to her. She is still the same person, she remains true to her former self. Despite the fact that the main half has gone out of her life, she remains incurious as to motives. She does not now begin to look below the surface. So, even under the stress of her knowledge about Stevie's death, she does not enquire into motives. She wishes to learn no more of the truth than the simple appearance of things.

"He took the boy away from me to murder him!" (p. 246).

Conrad also uses this sequence to increase the humanity of her being. Winnie has been so devoted to Stevie that even now, stunned as she is, and wretched at the news of her brother's death, she cannot adapt to life without him.

> This man was talking of going abroad. The impression was completely disconnected; and such is the force of mental habit that Mrs Verloc at once and automatically asked herself: "And what of Stevie?"
> It was a sort of forgetfulness; but instantly she became aware that there was no longer any occasion for anxiety on that score. There would never be any occasion any more. The poor boy had been taken out and killed. The poor boy was dead (p. 251).

Had Conrad not painted such a concise and brilliant portrayal of Winnie already, if we did not know that Stevie had become all that matters to her, we might reasonably suppose that this woman would experience a sense of freedom once the responsibility of looking after an idiot brother had been taken away. In a sense, this is exactly what she does experience, but the form that this freedom takes is not just that of a feeling of relief.

> At that precise moment Mrs Verloc began to look upon herself as released from all earthly ties. She had her freedom. Her contract with existence, as represented by that man standing over there, was at an end. She was a free woman (p. 251).

The freedom that Winnie experiences is that "from all earthly ties". Her mother has become virtually a foreigner to her, the necessity of maintaining allegiance to her husband no longer exists. So her freedom means freedom from Verloc, and from any earthly systems of morality or any social code. This clearly derives in part from the utilitarian purpose, that of caring for Stevie, with which Winnie undertook this particular marriage. But more than this it stems from the fact already mentioned that their marriage has never been a true marriage. Its very foundation has been one of misguided deceit, for Verloc believed he was loved for himself, while Winnie saw him as a means of stabilising Stevie's future.

The earthly ties, as I have just now suggested, also embrace the notion of an earthly morality, which Winnie no longer feels at all bound by, hence the form of her retaliation in taking a life for a life. This is not to say that Winnie rationalises the situation and consciously opts in favour of a 'natural' or 'absolute' morality rather than the socially accepted one for London. Victim as she is of her own family circumstances, she becomes open to the merest suggestion, to any way out, like a female animal deprived of its young in the wild.

> But this creature, whose moral nature had been subjected to a shock of which, in the physical order, the most violent earthquake of history could only be a faint and languid rendering, was at the mercy of mere trifles, of casual contacts (p. 255).

This we may expect, not just in the light of her past conduct and motivation, but because Conrad has only recently warned that "she did not exactly know what use to make of her freedom" (p. 254).

To remind us that we are still in a situation that is entirely human and un-novelistic, Conrad again illustrates the poles the husband and wife are apart, continuing to symbolise the gulf that has divided them from the start by Verloc's not realising Winnie's reasons for marrying him. He believes that she is on the point of rushing away to her mother's. But as we know already, Winnie's divorce from her mother is not just in place, but a spiritual one also, and nothing is further from her thoughts. Throughout all his writing here, by subtle hints that belie the casual reader, Conrad stresses Winnie's sacrifice in marrying Verloc.

> This woman, capable of a bargain the mere suspicion of which would have been infinitely shocking to Mr Verloc's idea of love, remained irresolute, as if scrupulously aware of something wanting on her part for the formal closing of the transaction (p. 259).

The whole point of Verloc's existence is over as far as Winnie is concerned. Furthermore he has been the destruction of her second bid for happiness. The first she voluntarily rejected. The second involved Stevie's life. And as if this was itself passing through Winnie's mind at this juncture, she experiences a pictorial vision of Stevie's mangled body. So following the progression of her feelings, the breakdown of the bargain between herself and Verloc, then the need to conclude the transaction, comes the only way really to end it.

> Mrs Verloc's doubts as to the end of the bargain no longer existed; her wits, no longer disconnected, were working under the control of her will (p. 261).

With this realisation comes a fantastic change in Winnie. She is once more a creature of passion, but again with the instincts of the female animal, it is now a controlled passion containing cunning and guile. The situation is forcing her into a new role.

> She commanded her wits now, her vocal organs; she felt herself to be in an almost preternaturally perfect control of every fibre of her body. It was all her own because the bargain was at an end. She was clear sighted. She had become cunning. She chose to answer him so readily for a purpose. She did not wish that man to change his position on the sofa which was very suitable to the circumstances. She succeeded (p. 261).

This is no longer the docile Winnie who appeared behind the counter of the Brett Street shop to serve embarrassed male customers with a bottle of marking-ink. She has become the she-devil of her own childhood, still defending Stevie. However, the defence is not now aimed at their father but at Verloc. Winnie has truly become demoniac. She is possessed by Stevie, even to the extent of a physical similarity.

> As if the homeless soul of Stevie had flown for shelter straight to the breast of his sister, guardian, and protector, the resemblance of her face with that of her brother grew at every step, even to the droop of the lower lip, even to the slight divergence of the eyes (p. 262).

So Verloc is killed by Stevie as much as by Winnie, murdered by a passionate impulse arising from sheer despair and frustration. And Winnie breathes freely, if only for a short while.

> She had become a free woman with a perfection of freedom which left her nothing to desire and absolutely nothing to do, since Stevie's urgent claim on her devotion no longer existed. Mrs Verloc, who thought in images, was not troubled now by visions, because she did not think at all. And she did not move.

She was a woman enjoying her complete irresponsibility and endless leisure almost in the manner of a corpse. She did not move, she did not think. Neither did the mortal envelope of the late Mr Verloc reposing on the sofa. Except for the fact that Mrs Verloc breathed these two would have been perfectly in accord: that accord of prudent reserve without superfluous words, and sparing of signs, which had been the foundation of their respectable home life (pp. 263–4).

Together with this master touch of irony in showing their proximity, Conrad shows us too the completeness of Winnie's amorality here. It forms a pattern which coincides with the amorality manifested by Verloc in his use of Stevie. But whereas Verloc's mental indolence allowed his social conscience, or rather his awareness of how society might retaliate against him, to remain in ignorance, Winnie's sense of relief is short-lived. With the blood comes an awareness of legal pressure and an obsessive fear of the gallows.

(ix)

I have attempted to deal with the character of Winnie at the time of the two deaths in some detail because it seems to me to be an incomparable piece of writing. But more than this it illustrates Conrad's development of different facets of moralities within a human situation. Winnie is here both victim and exile. Her loneliness is really what causes her tragedy, as we shall see when we go on to examine the role of Ossipon at the end of the novel. But this loneliness is not just a result of her own family circumstances. It is caused by the whole environment of the novel, that is, by society at large. So that ultimately Conrad forces us to an acceptance of the fact that Winnie is a victim of society, no less than Verloc is a victim of his own attempts to remain indolently solvent.

But Winnie's story does not end at this. It is not just society as a vague concept that has victimised her. Individuals conspire against her. Even Stevie is in a sense the betrayer of his own sister, while Vladimir, Heat, Verloc, and her own mother all combine to make her position the more intolerable. To this list we can also add the vile Ossipon, for it is he who is the ultimate betrayer. Winnie's revenge, it should be remembered, had been "obscurely prompted" (p. 267). So there are no grounds on which she feels she could defend herself if the matter came to the issue.

> Mrs Verloc was no longer a person of leisure and irresponsibility. She was afraid. The stabbing of Mr Verloc had been only a blow. It had relieved the pent-up agony of shrieks strangled in her throat, of tears dried up in her hot eyes, of the maddening and indignant rage at the atrocious part played by that man who was less than nothing now, in robbing her of the boy. It had been an obscurely prompted blow (p. 267).

Never having enquired into motives herself, she allows her action to appear unmotivated in her own eyes. But her fear of the gallows, symbolised by the repetition of "The drop given was fourteen feet . . ." forces her to an attempt not at self-justification but escape. Being now utterly friendless, she fastens naturally enough on the idea of suicide by drowning. This is the situation when Ossipon, on a night-prowling attempt to "stick close to the woman", comes across her. Conrad here plays a cat-and-mouse game with the characters, allowing us some ironical relief while not relaxing the tension at all. For Ossipon still believes at first that Verloc himself, not Stevie, was the immediate victim of the explosion. In technical terms, the meeting with Ossipon allows Conrad an unusually complete statement of the novel's central tragedy. Winnie's outpouring is long, but it is so important that one must quote it in full.

> "Look here, Tom! I was a young girl. I was done up. I was tired. I had two people depending on what I could do, and it did seem as if I couldn't do any more. Two people—mother and the boy. He was much more mine than mother's. I sat up nights and nights with him on my lap, all alone upstairs, when I wasn't more than eight years old myself. And then—— He was mine. I tell you . . . You can't understand that. No man can understand it. What was I to do? There was a young fellow——"
>
> The memory of the early romance with the young butcher

survived, tenacious, like the image of a glimpsed ideal in that
heart quailing before the fear of the gallows and full of revolt
against death.

"That was the man I loved then," went on the widow of Mr
Verloc. "I suppose he could see it in my eyes, too. Five and twenty
shillings a week, and his father threatened to kick him out of the
business if he made such a fool of himself as to marry a girl with
a crippled mother and a crazy idiot of a boy on her hands. But he
would hang about me, till one evening I found the courage to
slam the door in his face. I had to do it. I loved him dearly. Five
and twenty shillings a week! There was that other man—a good
lodger. What is a girl to do? Could I've gone on the streets? He
seemed kind. He wanted me, anyhow. What was I to do with
mother and that poor boy? Eh? I said yes. He seemed good-
natured, he was free-handed, he had money, he never said anything. Seven years—seven years a good wife to him, the kind, the
good, the generous, the—— And he loved me. Oh, yes. He loved
me till I sometimes wished myself—— Seven years. Seven years
a wife to him. And do you know what he was, that dear friend of
yours? Do you know what he was? . . . He was a devil!" (pp.
275–6).

The whole story is contained in the above words. The whole
life of denial, and the long-remembered love that she once
again had to take the solitary and wretched decision over.
The whole speech is also made the more powerful by its being
delivered to Ossipon. Winnie believes herself loved by someone who will care for her and effect her escape. She has been
so blind as to motives in the past that now she is unable to
make the simplest accurate judgements about characters. She
clings to him as a "radiant messenger of life" (p. 274), and he
takes advantage of her at every opportunity, not even failing
to relieve her of her 'safe' banknotes.

At no point does Conrad let the suspense flag. Back at the
shop, where he at last discovers the truth of the situation,
Ossipon has to switch the gas off at the meter. And, further,
the testing of the door by the policeman on duty allows
Conrad both to maintain the tension and remind his readers
of Verloc's police agency. It is here too that we are confirmed
in our beliefs about the terrified Ossipon, the staunch anarchist editor of 'The Freedom of the Proletariat'.

He was so frightened that for a moment the insane notion of strangling her in the dark passed through his mind. And he became more frightened than ever! She had him! he saw himself living in abject terror in some obscure hamlet in Spain or Italy; till some fine morning they found him dead, too, with a knife in his breast— . . . (p. 291).

One must not overlook the scorn of Conrad's tone here. Here is the political protagonist faced with a domestic crisis, unable to cope with the individual whose lot he is supposed to be easing. Consequently, although Ossipon appears to be freed, first by his own leap from the train, and then by Winnie's suicide, Conrad purposely tells us of Ossipon's future.

Already his robust form, with an Embassy's secret-service money (inherited from Mr Verloc) in his pockets, was marching in the gutter as if in training for the task of an inevitable future. Already he bowed his broad shoulders, his head of ambrosial locks, as if ready to receive the leather yoke of the sandwich board (p. 311).

The last chapter has a much greater technical function, however, than merely that of gathering together the threads of the plot. We must of course learn of Winnie's death, and of Ossipon and the Professor. But more than this, it is from these last pages that Conrad finally enforces the moral schema of the novel, by allowing a general conversation to take place between the Professor and Ossipon. This is clearly the only technical reason for the inclusion of the Professor's dicta on Michaelis' biography, and on life in general. For it must be remembered that the Professor is the only real anarchist. In Conrad's concluding words he is "unsuspected and deadly". And although his aim is the production of the perfect detonator, he has a moral viewpoint that is worked out in relation to society as it actually exists rather than the abstract musings of the other anarchists in the novel. Of Michaelis he says,

"He has divided his biography into three parts, entitled—'Faith, Hope, Charity.' He is elaborating now the idea of a world planned out like an immense and nice hospital, with gardens and flowers, in which the strong are to devote themselves to the nursing of the weak" (p. 303).

56

This is a simple statement, but its relevance to *The Secret Agent* is absolutely paramount. What we must first of all understand is that within society strength and weakness are entirely relative. Compared with Stevie, Winnie has been strong, and her devotion to him can only be lauded. But once he has gone, her strength no longer exists and her position becomes the reverse. Compared to her, Ossipon is strong, but he is unable to make for her any sacrifices at all, let alone one of the proportions of that which Winnie has made for Stevie. Indeed, the whole book can be read in terms of the interplay between strength and weakness in different characters, and of the same characters in altering circumstances. The statement itself gives us however an absolute moral standard for judgement within the terms of the novel.

(x)

To deal with the actual events of Winnie's death, Conrad takes us further away from her personally, using again the delayed narrative technique. The power of the writing here lies in the use of the simple phrase like

as if she were in some awful trouble (p. 308)

with the ironic overtones of, for example, the journalist.

"An impenetrable mystery seems destined to hang for ever over this act of madness or despair" (p. 307).

The irony here lies in the simplicity of the mystery, and the power of the comment for us from its closing three words. It is also in the light of these words that Conrad can have his last say about Winnie, and he drives it home the further because it is recognised by Ossipon.

But Comrade Ossipon knew that behind that white mask of despair there was struggling against terror and despair a vigour of vitality, a love of life that could resist the furious anguish which drives to murder and the fear, the blind, mad fear of the gallows (p. 308).

57

Only from our knowledge of Winnie can we reject absolutely the Professor's analysis, his cold-hearted impersonal analysis of such human traits as madness and fear.

"There are no such things. All passion is lost now. The world is mediocre, limp, without force. And madness and despair are a force. And force is a crime in the eyes of the fools, the weak and the silly who rule the roost. . . . Madness and despair! Give me that for a lever, and I'll move the world" (p. 309).

We reject his dismissal of fear. But we are forced into an acknowledgement of the power of passion. Further we must yield to the fact that only in the eyes of fools has Winnie committed a crime. Thus she is the victim not just of individuals but of society at large which would have condemned her in her wretched bid for self-justification. This is the positive morality which the book enforces. Winnie's moral shortsightedness does not detract from it in any way. It allows her to be the greatest single moral force in the novel without having to manifest an overpowering goody-goodiness, or its reverse. Indeed the whole thing helps to reinforce the simplicity of her emotional needs. Her life is a compromise between loyalty to her family and finding an outlet for her passionate nature. She is the victim throughout; first of her father, then of her own volition, in her relationship with the butcher's boy. Her sacrifice has been without reward.

This way in which Conrad never leaves his readers in doubt as to his moral perspectives, even when so many of his characters behave either immorally or amorally, is perhaps the most remarkable of his achievements in *The Secret Agent*. The problem of the difference between what is believed to be right and what is really right is never allowed to cloud the issue, though it runs just below the surface right the way through the novel. Again, Conrad is not standing aloof and scorning man as if he were some Augustan satirist. He is himself within the body of mankind acknowledging what man is, showing the irony and the pathos, on a personal level, of the woman driven to anarchy by an anarchist who is really anti-anarchist. But he is doing rather more than this. He is looking into and questioning the moralities of individuals and the morality of society in general. As I hope to have shown, the men—let us for the moment except Stevie—are self-concerned. This is true of all the men; anarchists, diplomats and police. Even Verloc, despite his proclaimed vocation as a protector of society, is largely comfort-seeking, and has never even thought of enquiring into his wife's motives in marrying him. He is self-indulgence and complacency personified.

The positive moralities derive from Stevie, his mother and of course from Winnie. It need hardly be pointed out that of these three the most straightforward is Stevie. But he is an idiot, and he is destroyed. Society seems bent on complications. Simplicity must be exterminated, and the simple in outlook are not allowed to exist. To some extent this is the reason for Winnie's suicide. Of course one uses ˚the word simplicity here in no pejorative sense. The simplicity of her outlook is really what causes her downfall. It never allows her to justify self-indulgence. But both die because of the complications society forces around them, the intrigues, and the legal code. All the characters around this central trio are wily; they make sure that whatever the motive, the deed appears sound. This is even true of Verloc who, while protecting his easy manner of life, stages an outrage to pacify Vladimir. So the natural simplicities of Stevie and Winnie are no protection against the complexities of society. As members of society, their simplicity is non-conformist and they suffer. Innocence provides no exemption, for neither can opt out of society if he is to continue to live. It is the society which is corrupt and corrupts.

When Winnie performs such an anti-social action as murdering her husband, she at once becomes answerable to society. Although her behaviour may seem to her utterly justifiable in terms of the family context, and in terms of the sacrifice which she has herself made, she is forced to realise that as a member of society she needs to pay service to an acknowledged system of public morality. In this case, by the laws of the country, private must yield to public. This is the same equation as defeated Verloc. His public role is forced into action by Vladimir, and, having founded his life on a morality where his public self yields to his private comfort, he is thereby defeated.

It is of course not only in these sections of the novel that Conrad shows the conflicting relationship of public and private moral schemes. The police co-ordinate the two. Ossipon leads a life of public disdain for social morality, while privately acknowledging its sovereignty. And Verloc himself, as has been suggested, makes his biggest mistake in not doing what the Assistant Commissioner saw as being so important, that is, realising the connection between the two moralities, public and private, and forcing them to work together.

However, the matter goes still a bit further than this. Conrad's personal involvement leads him to write the following words in his Author's Note.

> I have no doubt, however, that there had been moments during the writing of the book when I was an extreme revolutionist, I won't say more convinced than they but certainly cherishing a more concentrated purpose than any of them had ever done in the whole course of his life. I don't say this to boast. I was simply attending to my business. In the matter of all my books I have always attended to my business. I have attended to it with complete self-surrender. And this statement, too, is not a boast. I could not have done otherwise. It would have bored me too much to make-believe (p. xiv).

This is what gives truly great fiction its greatness of course, the reality of the issues with which it deals. This also explains why the moral purpose is so important to Conrad. He is dealing all the time with reality, coping with genuine situations, and trying to show what is wrong with them. But the Author's Note is not just a statement of moral purpose. It is also a personal self-justification for Conrad.

> I have always had a propensity to justify my action. Not to defend. To justify. Not to insist that I was right but simply to explain that there was no perverse intention, no secret scorn for the natural sensibilities of mankind at the bottom of my impulses (p. viii).

So Conrad gives Winnie all the sympathy he has. She was behaving naturally. But more than this he tells us in the earlier quotation that we may not just look and pity. It is our concern; not so much the way Winnie's maternal passion works against the reality of the town in fighting against her circumstances and her environment, but more the way in which it works to inspire in us pity, scorn and, perhaps most important, indignation.

3

'Under Western Eyes'

(i)

U NDER Western Eyes has the most straightforward plot of the three novels discussed here. It is the story of Razumov, the quietly studious illegitimate son of a Russian prince. He becomes implicated in a political assassination by Haldin, a fellow undergraduate who has misinterpreted Razumov's scholarly withdrawal for political silence, and who has assumed that Razumov is a lone anarchist. Razumov, being unable through circumstances over which he can exert no control to assist Haldin's escape, reports him to the authorities who, after making the arrest, send Razumov as a political spy to Switzerland, that is to the very community of which Haldin's mother and sister are members. Here Razumov falls in love with the sister, and, unable to bear the falsehood of his position, betrays himself by confession.

In this novel, we can already see quite clearly that Conrad again treats the theme of exile, but here the spiritual exile of Razumov from his fellows is symbolised by the physical exile with which his life is punctuated. We first meet him as an apparently orphaned student, though in fact the natural son of a Russian aristocrat, exiled from his family, vainly hugging a university career as the sole source of his own personal security. As the plot advances, he becomes alienated, exiled from university, forced into an ethnic exile in Switzerland, and, as a result of being in this way bandied hither and thither, he becomes a victim of a breakdown in that moral perspicacity which had characterised his first actions as the centre of the novel. Hence, driven by love and lack of any moral support on which to rest, he betrays himself and becomes, as we shall see, the victim of one of Conrad's most masterly ironies at the hands of the Dame de Compagnie.

That, crudely, is the outline of the novel, but Conrad adds

a disinterested narration of considerable force by giving us as story-teller a sort of political Marlow in the person of the Professor of Languages. Conrad adequately justifies this outside intervention. This is in no way the Professor's story, not even as much as, let us say, *Lord Jim* is Marlow's story. But by using the delayed narrative technique, Conrad is able to bring a verisimilitude to bear on his material which he clearly fears a direct narration might lack.

> Wonder may be expressed at a man in the position of teacher of languages knowing all this with such definiteness. A novelist says this and that of his personagcs, and if only he knows how to say it earnestly enough he may not be questioned upon the inventions of his brain in which his own belief is made sufficiently manifest by a telling phrase, a poetic image, the accent of emotion. Art is great! But I have no art . . . (p. 162).

This is of course one of the supreme statements of Conrad's own art, for it combines a denial of fiction's contrivings with the modest assertion of impartiality. Indeed Conrad forces us to stop here as we read, and ponder. When a novelist claims that he is not writing a novel, what are we to make of it? Is there in this the sort of false modesty that amounts to a fishing for praise where none is really due? Our knowledge of the traumata Conrad suffered while writing his novels would clearly deny all this. Is it then a genuine request delivered directly to the reader for reassurance, a sincere asking for the reader's approval? Certainly there is here an echo of those doubts which seem to have haunted Conrad whenever he was in the act of creating. But why allow an expression of this very personal sentiment into the writing at all? Surely Conrad had enough self-control to exclude it if it conflicted with the artistic design of the book. The only answer is that it cannot have conflicted with Conrad's conception of *Under Western Eyes* as a work of art. First of all Conrad is identifying himself here with the Professor of Languages, and secondly he wants to make it quite clear that this character should not obtrude into the novel. This, however, still does not answer the problem why call a novel not a novel. As I have suggested in the previous chapter, Conrad's chief concern in his writings was not with their fictional quality, but with the fact that they dealt with genuine existing issues, dilemmas and quandaries. This is what *Under Western Eyes* is about. Hence his denial in another place that this is a work of imagination. The Professor is a character within the novel. Hence what goes on inside the framework of the novel is real to him. He is also Conrad, for whom the work of fictional art remains a similar reality. Whether we accept *Under Western Eyes* as a novel or not is clearly up to us and the way we read, but we will clearly be more in accord with Conrad's intentions and with what he wishes of us if we treat it at its face value as a genuine narrative, within the framework that we loosely call fiction, but of real importance, where 'real' means the opposite of 'fiction'.

We can find support for this elsewhere where Conrad, still using the persona of the Professor of Languages, comments on the difficulty of using fiction to promote an entirely serious moral hypothesis.

> Words, as is well known, are the great foes of reality. I have been for many years a teacher of languages. It is an occupation which at length becomes fatal to whatever share of imagination, observation, and insight an ordinary person may be heir to. To a teacher of languages there comes a time when the world is but a place of many words and man appears a mere talking animal not much more wonderful than a parrot (p. 3).

This is the narrator's personal view of reality. He sees men as reduced virtually to the status of robots, and he can report only what he hears and sees. Hence his own impressions, since they can report nothing more than what actually went on, will need analysis and interpretation, and this must come from the reader himself. The narrator will give us only the barest minimum, and, in so doing, will provide only the skeleton of the story. This is what Conrad is telling us here, though we may not be prepared to believe him. He wants us to realise that our emotions are not going to be manipulated. He is going to state the incidents and be amoral as to any conclusions. The decisions about good and bad, and about right and wrong, are entirely our own. But Conrad does not pretend that he is creating a novel without outlook, or without viewpoint, even discounting for the moment the moral one. For the Professor's are the Western Eyes under which the machinations of the Easterners, aristocrats and anarchists alike, are scanned.

> In its pride of numbers, in its strange pretensions of sanctity, and in the secret readiness to abase itself in suffering, the spirit of Russia is the spirit of cynicism (p. 67).

This embodies the whole of Conrad's attitude towards Russia and summarises his hatred of all that is Russian. It also gives us a précis of those national traits which will provide the stepping stones for the development of the novel. It begins with the reference to the sheer physical size of the Russian nation in terms of people, and moves to voluntary suffering. In just the same way the novel begins with the tacit assertion that might is right and moves to voluntary self-inflicted martyrdom. Cynicism, it has been written, is the last refuge of the idealist. In Conrad's analysis of the spirit of Russia it is not quite the last. The irony of the false existence, which Conrad claimed was the lot of those who lived the life on shore, has something else in store.

But this does not stop him from reminding us, time and time again, of the reality of Razumov's situation. In a sense, as has been suggested, this is done symbolically, in the first place by his underlining of the differences between this work and a novel. But he also does it by what must amount to one of the most confident assertions of an author's self-doubt in fiction.

> A grain of talent excuses many faults. But this is not a work of imagination; I have no talent; my excuse for this undertaking lies not in its art, but in its artlessness. Aware of my limitations and strong in the sincerity of my purpose, I would not try (were I able) to invent anything. I push my scruples so far that I would not even invent a transition (p. 100).

It is easy to overlook the full implications of these words. They are more than a comment from Conrad to us, at worst a statement of inadequacy, or at best of overmodest self-assessment. They provide a complete character portrayal of the

Professor. The mention of scruples has the ring of absolute sincerity. None the less he is a pedantic and in many ways rather pathetic little observer. The point is not that he is pedantic, but that he is scrupulous to the minutest degree. Furthermore, the basis of his scruples is both simple and well founded. It is sure. He is, in other words, morally sound, and the significance of this lies in the fact that his whole ethical creed is incredibly simple. He corresponds in the extent of this simplicity with the characters who in *Chance* are called the Sea Set. He provides a sort of moral anchor here for the vagaries of the other characters in the novel. It is dangerous to try to draw parallels between different novelists' treatment of characters, for there frequently arises the temptation to try to take these parallels too far. It is not uncommon for students to justify Esther's role in *Bleak House* solely in terms of the novel's moral schemata. If she is the moral centre-piece around whom the rest of the novel fluctuates, in and out in a constantly altering spiral, one can only admire Conrad's genius the more for having provided us in *Under Western Eyes* with a central moral norm who is entirely human and who does not manifest any of Esther's overpowering and almost divine perfection in moral terms.

This Professor provides the mode of narration by which Conrad, while insisting that we have complete freedom to make moral judgements on the characters of the novel in our own way, in fact shackles us, his readers, to an absolute single moral point of view. Conrad again uses his formula of birth, suffering and death. Razumov fully experiences all of these, both physically and spiritually. In the beginning, he is not an uncommon type of character. He fits very simply indeed into Conrad's universal picture of humanity as it was in 1911.

> . . . what all men are really after is some form or perhaps only some formula of peace. Certainly they are crying loud enough for it at the present day (p. 5).

Given his lack of family circumstances, Razumov only wants to be left alone to work out for himself a successful student career, and in this chapter it is my purpose to show how Conrad easily turns this particular member of a suffering humanity into another Verloc, or rather into a creature with moral affinities to Verloc, but in a different private situation. It should not be necessary to point out that the word private is used here in its moral sense. The circumstances of both Verloc and Razumov are much the same, and despite their differences in their choices of action, because both lack a true and simple moral orientation, the end results of their actions are not dissimilar. Razumov's career, as it interests us, runs through a series of separate influencing factors, but initially, as has already been mentioned, his need is the basic human one, though here accentuated by his being both particularly sensitive and illegitimate. Having come into contact with Haldin's personal anarchy, he chooses to betray this to the government for purely selfish reasons and is thus compromised into becoming a secret agent (hence another similarity between him and Verloc). While in close contact with the anarchists, significantly on neutral territory in Switzerland, he suffers various heightened forms of exile; he has of course firstly been exiled from a university career by the government as a result of his action. Naturally as a result of this he moves into an environment of greater anarchism than even that of the university, for he must, as a part of his mission, join in the life of a group of supposedly active anarchists. Naturally enough he feels alienated from this micro-society, membership of which has been forced upon him. Finally he is forced by his own temperament, and by falling in love with Haldin's sister[1], to betray himself by confessing everything to her and to the anarchical group as a whole. This is a further final exile for it not only betrays him, but also the trust that has been bestowed on him by the government, and so he becomes alienated spiritually as well as physically from his father, who symbolises here the Russian Authorities. So, briefly, he begins as a voluntary exile from his fellow students—in modern Oxford parlance,

---

[1] Conrad uses Natalia or Nathalie almost at random when writing of Miss Haldin, and there is even inconsistency between editions. For the sake of simplification I have used the Anglicised form Nathalie throughout, except in quotations where I retain the reading of the Dent Collected Edition.

a 'Grey Man'—joins the authorities by betraying his friend, and finally is himself betrayed not just by the Authorities, but by his own actions and through the amorality of his outlook.

(ii)

If we are to consider next the first of these influences on Razumov, we must turn to his life at the university and to the figure of Haldin. Since this latter passes fleetingly through the novel, he need not detain us long. He is, it need hardly be said, the exact opposite of the anarchists in *The Secret Agent*, working not for his own comfort but motivated by deeply-felt convictions. None the less he gains some measure of both excitement and pleasure from the consequences of his bomb-throwing.

> No doubt he was looking forward to the consummation of his martyrdom. A man who resigns himself to kill need not go very far for resignation to die. Haldin slept perhaps more soundly than General T—, whose task—weary work too—was not done, and over whose head hung the sword of revolutionary vengeance (p. 70).

Conrad's tone is important here for, beside the colloquial ring of "—weary work too—", we can appreciate why Conrad stresses the resignation in Haldin's attitude. No man as sympathetic and intelligent as Haldin enjoys killing, but the firmness of his convictions, and the grounding of his moral position, force him to do so. He is overcome by the fervour of his belief.

> "Your brother believed in the power of a people's will to achieve anything?"
> "It was his religion," declared Miss Haldin (p. 133).

Against the selfless positivism of this moral outlook, Razumov measures, as we shall see in due course, but poorly. Haldin offers us, in his fleeting appearances in the novel, the height of disinterested selflessness and provides an immediate contrast with the civil servants and aristocrats whose own appearances are alternated with Haldin's to considerable effect.

One must of course appreciate that these members of the government and government offices are far more embroiled in the actual system of the state than ever Haldin was. In many ways, they are far less their own masters than he. It is however in their attitudes to Razumov that the difference appears most markedly. Haldin, it is true, has not been over-considerate of Razumov's personal safety. But then he has not been over-considerate of his own either. Furthermore, he is of the firm conviction that Razumov is a fellow conspirator, who would therefore be more than eager to help him. His sin, if such it is, is one of mistaken judgement, not, as with the Authorities, in the clear-sighted manipulation of supposedly free-acting persons. For this is of course exactly what they do to Razumov.

> It seems that the savage autocracy, no more than the divine democracy, does not limit its diet exclusively to the bodies of its enemies. It devours its friends and servants as well (p. 306).

Conrad shows the whole system of government as inappropriate to the needs of the people,

> But was it not sin enough to live on a government salary while half Russia was dying of hunger? The Ministry of Finances! What a grotesque horror it is! What does the starving, ignorant people want with a Ministry of Finances? (p. 150),

and unscrupulous in its use of individuals. The moment Razumov turns informer, he is committed to lead the rest of his life as the tool of autocracy, and the victim of General T—'s hypocrisy. Even while the general says to Razumov "Nobody doubts the moral soundness of your action" (p. 47), he is assessing Razumov's usefulness particularly as a pawn, one of the secret agents of his spy ring.

> "I am interested in him. He has, it seems, the great and useful quality of inspiring confidence" (p. 49).

But this does not prevent the general from treating Razumov with the gravest suspicion and from initiating the course of events which begins with the rifling of Razumov's room, and results in his being sent to Switzerland by Mikulin and incidentally being exiled from the university where he had hoped to become an eminent professor.

(iii)

Switzerland provides Conrad with a magnificent setting for a group of anarchists whose active lives do not differ greatly from those who appear in *The Secret Agent*, all of whom provide such a splendid contrast with Haldin. His behaviour, as we have seen, was the result of disinterested conviction while theirs stemmed from comfort-seeking selfishness. Indeed they, together with Razumov, are searching largely for some measure of peace in their lives. Where the difference really lies is that Razumov has the honesty not to pretend that he is anything but what he actually is. Indeed, his whole conduct is marked by the honest self-scrutiny to which he subjects himself and which causes his downfall.

The anarchists whom Conrad has assembled for us in Switzerland are totally otherwise.

> . . . —in a real revolution the best characters do not come to the front. A violent revolution falls into the hands of narrow-minded fanatics and of tyrannical hypocrites at first. Afterwards comes the turn of all the pretentious intellectual failures of the time. Such are the chiefs and leaders. You will notice that I have left out the mere rogues. The scrupulous and the just, the noble, humane and devoted natures; the unselfish and intelligent may begin a movement—but it passes away from them. They are not the leaders of a revolution. They are its victims; . . . (p. 134).

So Razumov becomes the observer of such as these. But we would be wrong to assume that Conrad is showing us stereotypes. Indeed, with typical irony, he shows us a group, ostensibly led by Peter Ivanovitch, the Great Feminist, where the women gain our sympathy very much more than the men. Indeed the whole character of Peter Ivanovitch, who worked out his philosophy of the Great European Powers while tramping the bogs of Siberia, is worthy of consideration. He it is who provides the greatest single aspect of irony in the novel, for it is he who unwittingly analyses Razumov's predicament for us when, having advocated his belief in the power of women, he points out that "Knowledge in itself is mere dross" (p. 120). He also indicates, through his past life, woman's spiritual and physical superiority in that he was freed from his chains by a girl who had trudged across Russia to be with her lover who had died before she arrived. So he has become a not-so-noble savage, until he is finally cared for by Mme de S— at the incredible Château Borel. In fact this location provides a magnificent example of what Professor Gurko calls Conrad's Ecology (v. Leo Gurko, *Joseph Conrad, Giant in Exile*, London, 1965, ch. ix, pp. 163–81). Conrad uses the Château to symbolise the anarchy of the Swiss group and to contrast it with Haldin's attempt. When we first see it, it is utterly empty inside except for the voice which no one is answering, which indeed no one hears except an outsider. This is the nature of the cause to which such as Laspara and Nikita/Necator, himself a secret agent, have allied themselves. Claiming that they are striving for the betterment of the people, they ignore the very voice of the people. As for Peter Ivanovitch, he is

the greatest genius of the century perhaps, but he is the most inconsiderate man living (p. 146),

and this shows the hiatus that exists in all of them, the difference between the assumed pose and the real person. Ivanovitch's pose can best be illustrated by a further quotation.

"Don't you understand that Peter Ivanovitch must direct, inspire, influence? It is the breath of his life. There can never be too many disciples. He can't bear thinking of anyone escaping him. And a woman, too! There is nothing to be done without women, he says. He has written it. He——" (p. 237).

Conrad is doing more than subjecting Ivanovitch to an ironic treatment here. The *double-entendre* in Ivanovitch's anarchical necessity for women, and Conrad's narrator's comment on their biological function in "There is nothing to be done without women" is only half the story. When it actually comes down to Ivanovitch's motives, we can realise the shallowness, the utter shallowness, of his moral conviction. He hopes for an assured and secure old age as the heir of Mme de S—, a hope which, incidentally, is not fulfilled, while towards a woman like Tekla, the ardent and misunderstood Dame de Compagnie in the Château Borel, his attitude both has been and still is one of absolute contempt. He is a *poseur*, and, together with all men, is only seeking "some form or perhaps some formula of peace". He is really the opposite of what he pretends to be, "an awful despot", who is, as Razumov himself sees, only sticking by Mme de S— to get at her money. So he ends, still an 'inspired man' married to a peasant girl, and the cycle of his so-called active life is completed. For his wife is clearly exactly the counterpart of the peasant girl who had tramped in vain across Russia, and who lent him the file to free himself. He symbolises supremely for us the dichotomy between the public and private moral schemes. His pose is really nothing more than lip-service. He assumes a public morality of non-acceptance which is really no more than a cover for his self-indulgence. Hence, in an individual context, the pattern of his private morality is indefensible. He has neither courage nor indeed any true convictions save those of looking after himself. So he fades out of the arena of the novel, rejected even by Mme de S—.

(iv)

Conrad is less harsh in his treatment of the women at the Château Borel. The ghoulish Mme de S— rules over them all with an air of decadent aristocracy. But she does not really concern us. Apart from Tekla, about whom more will be said shortly, we find our interests centring on Sophia Antonovna. She alone of the declared anarchists shows any concern for the human condition, and for the suffering individual. While still believing that Razumov was Haldin's political comrade, sympathising over Haldin's death, she says to Razumov

> "Don't I know how it feels after losing a comrade in the good fight? One's ashamed of being left. And I can remember so many. Never mind. They shall be avenged before long. And what is

death? At any rate, it is not a shameful thing like some kinds of life."

Razumov felt something stir in his breast, a sort of feeble and unpleasant tremor.

"Some kinds of life?" he repeated, looking at her searchingly.

"The subservient, submissive life . . ." (p. 260).

She is, of course unwittingly, goading and tormenting Razumov while attempting to do the opposite for him, just as her "crimson blouse being a flaring safety signal" (p. 265) inverts the true nature of the red warning signal. None the less, it is from her that the Professor of Languages learns the concluding chapters of Razumov's story, and it is from her too that Razumov gains forgiveness for the part he played in Haldin's downfall.

She is perhaps too gentle for an anarchist. For her convictions pale beside those of Tekla, for whom Conrad reserves his greatest commendations. Tekla is the personification of struggling humanity, labouring on unthanked, or, worse still, ignored, and it is she who, in blindness and ignorance, cares for Razumov through the last months of his life. She is the stereotype of the woman who must have a cause, caring for others or for the individual even if, as when we first meet her, the individual is a cat. Of course this is not to suggest that cats and people are the same to Tekla. They might have been to Peter Ivanovitch, but then he is much less aware, despite his own personal sufferings, of the needs of humanity than is Tekla.

> "Animals have their right; though, strictly speaking, I see no reason why they should not suffer as well as human beings. Do you? But of course they never suffer so much. That is impossible. Only, in their case it is more pitiful because they cannot make a revolution" (p. 147).

Her nature makes her the ideal companion for an ardent anarchist, but instead she is passed over by the Château Borel group.

> "While there are travellers ready to fall by the way our Tekla will never be idle. She is a good Samaritan by an irresistible vocation. The revolutionists didn't understand her. Fancy a

devoted creature like that being employed to carry about documents sewn in her dress, or made to write from dictation."
"There is not much perspicacity in the world" (p. 374).

Only Razumov sees her natural usefulness for his own particular concern.

> He understood that the bitterness accumulated in the heart of that helpless creature had got into her veins and, like some subtle poison, had decomposed her fidelity to that hateful pair. It was a great piece of luck for him, he reflected . . . She would be a good ally (p. 235).

Consequently he cultivates her friendship and it provides a further irony that this does turn out to be "a piece of luck for him" though not for the obtaining of useful political information.

On her part Tekla at first has her doubts about Razumov.

> "I don't know who that young man is to whom Peter Ivanovitch has taken such a fancy. He must be one of us, or he would not be admitted here when the others come. You know what I mean by the others. But I must say that he is not at all mystically inclined. I don't know that I have made him out yet" (p. 159).

These words, addressed to Nathalie Haldin, show Tekla as clearly having more awareness of the depths of human nature than any other person in the novel. It is probably because of this that she is one of the few true anarchists in the book. Furthermore she is ardent in her belief in anarchy, and, naturally therefore, longs for the overthrow of autocracy. Her moral position is a simple one, and her sincere beliefs are, unlike Ivanovitch's, in accordance with it. If governments are to exist, innocent people must suffer. That is the summary of her political and therefore public outlook. On a private and personal level, she has sacrificed herself in looking after the journeyman lithographer, and has lived a life of hell among the revolutionaries. Hers is the greatest living sacrifice of any of the characters in *Under Western Eyes*. She has never felt that she was very useful, and yet the chief misery within her philosophy of life is that of having nothing to look forward to. Consequently she provides us with the most interesting moral focus of any of the anarchists, and the one which Conrad most applauds. For with her it is not just a case of an amoral outlook, of never having examined her moral position, or of never trying or seeing the need for reconciling public morality with private. She asserts that morality is never a complete way of life. Personal relationships are important as well. So, despite his lack of mystical inclination, Razumov manages to reach her on a personal level. Later in the novel she says to him

> "It was your humane manner . . . I have been starving for, I won't say kindness, but just for a little civility, for I don't know how long" (p. 233).

The anarchists have been blind to the suffering in literally their own house. So she has appeared to them as a nonentity, a tool, rather than a human being, and so it is that she will seize any chance to respond to Razumov on a personal level.

> ". . . if you were to get ill . . . or meet some bitter trouble, you would find I am not a useless fool. You have only to let me know. I will come to you" (p. 233).

So it is that Tekla finds a reward, and a meaning in life, in nursing the deaf and crippled Razumov. We must remember too that she is never disillusioned about Razumov. Even when she is nursing him alone at the end of the novel, indeed beyond the end of the novel, she still believes that he was Haldin's confidant in the bomb-throwing incident. This shows us just how much Conrad approved of her. He allows her to achieve a sense of fulfilment in looking after what remains of an active anarchist. There is not a grain of true knowledge given her to spoil her happiness. She never learns the true nature of Razumov's appearance in Switzerland. So she can devote herself to him in the belief that he is still the hero she took him for, and can find reward and happiness in so doing. Incidental to doing this, she will also be alleviating more suffering than any of the Borel anarchists had ever done. Of her nursing of Razumov, Conrad tells us that "there was nothing in that task to become disillusioned about" (p. 379), particularly when her very existence has been illusion.

She—in the same way as we shall later see Nathalie Haldin do—ends up by performing what is to Conrad's mind woman's function in society, and this provides its own rewards. She has made no stance, has adopted no hypocritical pose, and consequently her life, in the last analysis, finds a purpose and a fulfilment on an entirely personal level, human being to human being. This is the height of her achievement.

These are Conrad's Swiss anarchists, a disreputable group of men with two redeeming women. There is, however, a unanimity in their opinion that slavishness is the main trouble with Russia. But in general they lack the self-knowledge of Tekla, and fail to realise that they are themselves subjecting others to slavery. There is as little equality in the Château Borel as there was in autocratic Russia. Peter Ivanovitch himself yields to the allure of aristocracy when he points out that a "leader . . . cannot come from the dregs of the people" (p. 211). These, he says, must remain at the bottom, and thus he denies the democracy whose coming he is supposed to be hastening. His whole philosophy rests on his confusion as to what constitutes the dregs of the people. Certainly the peasantry are not the dregs; nor, for that matter, are the nobility, the Prince K—s and the Councillor Mikulins. The dregs are formed from everything that is not genuine. Ivanovitch is right about this, but, perhaps wisely, he fails to follow the argument through to its logical conclusion. For Conrad's unstated comment is that the dregs of a people gather together at places like the Château Borel.

(v)

Despite Conrad's approval of Tekla, she lacks the advantages of Nathalie Haldin's youth and sweetness. Miss Haldin's influence on Razumov in Switzerland is therefore of a rather different nature, for, although his relationship with her is as disastrous to him as is his contact with the anarchists, she tends to hold aloof from the secret conclaves at the Château Borel. It is to Nathalie, then, that we must now turn our attention. One could not do less justice to Conrad than by assuming that she is merely a technically convenient link between the Professor of Languages and Razumov, inserted in order to make the narrative more natural by supplying the narrator with information which he could not otherwise be expected to possess. She does do this of course, but there is nothing nearly so clumsy in Conrad's manipulation of this particular plot. Nathalie's part is as integral as Tekla's, for it is she who finally heightens Razumov's despair into self-betrayal, and she does this by the sweetness of her character which one would expect to achieve just the opposite effect. So she contrasts sharply with her mother who

> was one of those natures, rare enough, luckily, in which one cannot help being interested, because they provoke both terror and pity. One dreads their contact for oneself, and still more for those one cares for, so clear it is that they are born to suffer and to make others suffer, too. It is strange to think that, I won't say liberty, but the mere liberalism of outlook which for us is a matter of words, of ambitions, of votes (and if of feeling at all, then of the sort of feeling which leaves our deepest affections untouched) may be for other beings very much like ourselves and living under the same sky, a heavy trial of fortitude, a matter of tears and anguish and blood (p. 318).

Miss Haldin stands outside her mother's beliefs, both political and otherwise. Her life she leads on a purely personal level. Indeed it is refreshing to have come across someone in the novel who does this. None the less, she is not an unthinking creature. In a sense, she seeks some sort of divinity to worship, though her expression of this never becomes more than a whimsical utterance.

> "The whole world is inconceivable to the strict logic of ideas. And yet the world exists to our senses, and we exist in it. There must be a necessity superior to our conceptions (p. 106).

Her life pivots on the characters of her mother and her brother, and the feeling that makes this so is of course reciprocated. Indeed it is through Haldin's concern for his family's welfare that his mother and sister are safely ensconced in Switzerland, and there is no doubt in the anti-Russian mind of his mother that his disappearance is the result of an auto-

77

cratic *coup*. So when her fears are finally verified by a newspaper, and the effect even on Nathalie is "as if the shock had paralysed her moral resistance" (p. 111), she becomes a virtual recluse. Nathalie, however, has the stamina, moral as well as physical, to cope with the situation. She seeks the truth, and, in commenting on her brother's death, provides us unwittingly with an analysis of Razumov.

> He may have been betrayed by some false friend or simply by some cowardly creature (p. 117).

Later, when her relationship with Razumov is gaining in warmth, she encourages him because she wants "to remain faithful to his departed spirit" (p. 140). This gives Conrad a further opportunity to exploit the tremendous ironic possibilities of this situation. Nathalie, virtually for her brother's sake, allows Razumov to fall in love with her. But Razumov's love has arisen from a reaction to the hatred he feels for very nearly everything and everyone connected with the name of Haldin. So Nathalie unwittingly avenges her brother, for, as we know, it is Razumov's love for her, and the hatred of deceiving her which accompanies it, that forces him into a confession.

At first, as one might expect, Razumov is at considerable pains to avoid Haldin's relatives. But this only serves to increase Nathalie's sympathy for him and the justification of his conduct. When they do meet, it is she who initiates all the action.

> It was only her outstretched hand which brought about the recognition. It stands recorded in the pages of his self-confession, that it nearly suffocated him physically with an emotional reaction of hate and dismay, as though her appearance had been a piece of accomplished treachery (p. 167).

So their knowledge of Haldin becomes a bond between them. But it is a bond which rests on ignorance and misapprehension. The Professor takes us some of the way towards appreciating this.

> I understood well enough that all their conversations must have been referred mentally to that dead man who had brought them together. That was unavoidable (p. 201).

On the one hand Razumov, through his hatred of Haldin's having forced him to leave the university, resents the very presence of the Haldins, while Nathalie suspects herself unworthy of association with her brother's friend. She has realised, not knowing that Razumov feels utterly hemmed in by his past, that he is 'observing' and 'studying' her, but, in accordance with her nature, she believes that it is to see whether she is "worthy of his trust".

As one would expect, the presence of the Haldins among the Russian population in Geneva yields grounds for great hope among the Borel group. Temperamentally Nathalie seems to us entirely unsuitable for a Maude Gonne type of activity, but this is not taken into account by the anarchists. She is the sister of the hero of the hour. To their eyes that is the first point in her favour. Secondly, of course, Peter Ivanovitch *must* have disciples. So much of their anarchical activity is an attempt at persuading Nathalie to join the group. It is to this end that they encourage Razumov's friendship with her. Only one of them, it seems, does not want to turn her into a second Mme de S——. This, once again, is Tekla, who orders Razumov not to bring her. She, let it be remembered, retains some sense of individual values. So she does not want Nathalie as well to become disillusioned. At least, she must not become Peter Ivanovitch's quarry.

This she is indeed spared, largely by her forcing Razumov's confession to the anarchists, and by her receiving of his diary. His confession to her is in fact probably what saves her from a life of so-called anarchy at the Château Borel. The change in her is overwhelming and immediate. At first she is reduced to the same state as her mother "who seemed to watch a beloved head lying in her lap" (p. 355).

Her hands were lying lifelessly, palms upwards, on her lap. She raised her grey eyes slowly. Shadows seemed to come and go in them as if the steady flame of her soul had been made to vacillate at last in the cross currents of poisoned air from the corrupted dark immensity claiming her for its own, where virtues themselves fester into crimes in the cynicism of oppression and revolt (p. 356).

There is a simplicity in her reply to Razumov's confession

"It is impossible to be more unhappy" (p. 356), that makes us sympathise the more with her suffering. But there are two redeeming features about it which grant a strength of sincerity to her subsequent actions, in much the same way as occurs in the case of Tekla. She is spared an existence founded on falsehood, and she is saved from the clutches of Peter Ivanovitch. When we finally again hear news of her, it is to learn that she is doing good social work in visiting jails and homes. Society is at last being allowed to benefit from the sweetness of her temperament and nature. Of these it would have been robbed had she joined the gathering at the Château Borel. So Nathalie too suffers a sort of redemption, for she ends up serving the needs of the people more than do any of those wrapped up in political activities. Where Tekla alleviates suffering in the particular, Nathalie does so in general. Her nature may perhaps be said to lack the power of Tekla's, but at least it has strength enough to withstand the bitterness of the truth.

(vi)

At this point we must turn to Razumov himself. *Under Western Eyes* is his story much more than either *Nostromo* or *The Secret Agent* is the story of any single character. His role in the novel is entirely central, for at no time does he yield up the centre of interest. This is his story more than that of any other individual, including Nathalie, and so it is on his character and conduct that we must now focus in detail. All Conrad's sympathies are directed towards him, and it is in the awareness of this that we should recall the words of the Author's Note.

> Razumov is treated sympathetically. Why should he not be? He is an ordinary young man, with a healthy capacity for work and sane ambitions. He has an average conscience. If he is slightly abnormal it is only in his sensitiveness to his position. Being nobody's child he feels rather more keenly than another would that he is a Russian—or he is nothing (p. ix).

Razumov's character is not nearly so difficult to understand as many critics would have us believe. On the simplest level one can see that he falls in love because, having never experienced that sense of belonging which grows out of the privilege of living as a member of the family unit, he needs more than most the love and security which his illegitimacy has always denied him, and which his father has tried to replace at first purely by financial aid, and secondly with political manipulation. His great misfortune—and it is so great that it almost amounts to a sort of *hubris* on his part—like that of so many of Conrad's heroes, is the misfortune of environment. But more than just this, it is the misfortune of personal circumstances in a hostile world, of personal alienation, even once more of exile. Because of all this, his betrayal is a betrayal of self brought about by his unfitness to cope with conditions in which his birth has forced him to live. Not just his birth, but the illegitimacy of it, combine to form his destiny. Every one of his choices of action can be referred back to the isolation of his situation, where family circumstances would have conditioned him to react quite differently.

Nowhere is all this more apparent than in the university scenes of the novel. When we first come into contact with him, Razumov is presented to us with an almost wraith-like quality. We can gain only a blurred image of his physical appearance, and the whole of his personality is summed up in two generalisations which, we soon learn, are like so many other generalisations in coming nowhere near the truth about the man:

he was easily swayed by argument and authority (p. 5),

and

his quiet readiness to oblige his comrades even at the cost of personal inconvenience (p. 6).

None the less, it is these two traits whose immediate conflict provides the drama on which *Under Western Eyes* depends, for the latter sends him out to Ziemianitch so that he may be of assistance to Haldin, while the former ultimately forces him to Geneva as a political pawn.

In dealing with Razumov the student, Conrad stresses that he is the child of Russia, rather than of a specific father. Indeed this is clearly one of the dramatic and artistic functions of his bastardy within the framework of the novel. We are not allowed to puzzle at all over the person of his father. Conrad makes this absolutely clear from a very early stage, though in the discreetest of terms. A further function here of course is that the loneliness caused by his family circumstances gives his whole studentship a seriousness and an intensity it might otherwise lack. It also acts as a catalyst upon his driving urge for recognition which derives from his knowledge of his father having been an aristocrat, is made the more acute by his longing to be able to acknowledge his sisters and to be acknowledged by them, and finally resolves itself into the ambition to become a celebrated professor which, at the commencement of the novel, is actuating him to write a prize-winning essay. Thus his immediate reaction to Haldin's confession is, as one would expect, one of dismay. But what is more interesting is that this dismay stems not from the nature of the confession but from the fact that the in-bursting of Haldin has interrupted the work on the crucial essay. This aside, one can already begin to see with what dramatic contriving Conrad has made Razumov a bastard, for on this one simple fact the whole personality evolves. But more than this, it provides, as I hope to have made clear, the whole environment for the novel, as well as its dramatic power.

What has been written above is in no way meant to detract from the politics of the situation. Conrad comments with a certain amount of pride that no one in England could have been forced into Razumov's position. But as soon as one begins to look at the novel as a political proposition, one moves away from the true centre of the work of art which concentrates on the individual. This is not to say that there are no political feelings in Conrad's writings. If there were not, one could barely justify his choice of a title for this particular novel; but one must not let the politics of the situation blind one to the dilemma of the individual. Conrad is playing these two against each other when he writes, in the early pages of *Under Western Eyes,*

> But consider that the true destroyers are they who destroy the spirit of progress and truth, not the avengers who merely kill the bodies of the persecutors of human dignity (p. 19).

He is already thinking of the fusion of public and private morality which together go to make up what is good; and he follows this up with thoughts on the personal side of morality which are going to be so utterly crucial to Razumov. It is of course important to notice that Razumov never doubts that his quandary is a moral one. There is little trouble from the concept of amorality in this work. However, showing considerable foresight, this is what he ponders.

> "What is betrayal? They talk of a man betraying his country, his friends, his sweetheart. There must be a moral bond first. All a man can betray is his conscience. And how is my conscience engaged here; by what bond of common faith, of common conviction, am I obliged to let that fanatical idiot drag me down with him? On the contrary—every obligation of true courage is the other way" (pp. 37–8).

In many ways this is the turning point which really makes Razumov Conrad's hero, and, as one would expect, there are several things to notice here. Razumov's lack of real experience, that is, his ignorance of the world, coupled to the fact that he has had little opportunity for establishing personal relationships, and thus simply of getting to know about people, leads him to formulate a distressingly naïve judgement in this particular situation. He comes down at once on the side of such a hopelessly vague concept as 'true courage' without halting for one moment over the problem of definition. This is a very fair indication which Conrad gives us as to the nature of Razumov's increasing quandary. His lack of background, his isolation, as it were, draws from him positive and unquestioning answers where there still remains a great deal of room for doubt. How can he be sure that what he thinks is right in this instance, now, really will be right in all its consequences? This lack of pondering does not amount to amorality on his part, but it is the nearest thing to it that morality can ever come. Similarly, this naïveté engenders in him a mental attitude by which he is quite unable, at this stage at any rate, to follow an action through to its conclusion. He is unable to see one move ahead, or even to realise the implications of the present action. So his immediate impulse is to go out to the assistance of Haldin.

It is Razumov's reactions to the different episodes in which he exists that are of most interest to us in *Under Western Eyes*. Razumov, as has already been remarked, feels resentment at Haldin's implicating him in his own folly, but this is more for interrupting the academic work in hand than because of the political imbroglio. Thus Haldin's care for Razumov's safety does nothing to appease the latter. Conrad drives home the force of this by commenting on how Razumov, making his way to the drunken Ziemianitch on his journey of salvation for Haldin, envies a beggarwoman "the peace of her mind and the serenity of her fate" (p. 27). Similarly his beating of Ziemianitch is a typically human reaction, again showing Conrad's insight into the human condition. Razumov uses his strength and takes advantage of Ziemianitch's stupor in order to relieve his own mental anguish and the sense of frustration pent up inside him. And having gained this physical satisfaction, he remains conscious only of hate. Suicide is no solution to him here, for he must extract himself from the coils of a political destiny which seem to be pulling him down from his one ambition, that of gaining recognition. It is yet another example of Conrad's mastery in exploiting an ironical situation that it is only when Razumov achieves recognition that his fate is utterly sealed.

His mission to Ziemianitch having failed, Razumov's isolation again increases his dilemma. He has, it seems, no one to turn to, his only relative being the cold, brutal, native earth of Russia. So the logic he takes as a guide is the logic of loyalty; but it is an argument whose rationality is tainted by egocentricity.

"If I must suffer let me at least suffer for my convictions, not for a crime my reason—my cool superior reason—rejects" (p. 35).

And it is in this state that he first experiences the hallucinatory vision of Haldin, a vision which, it should be noticed, is much more real to him than the crash of nearby sledges. This is barely a "cool, superior reason" at work. Unaware of the extent to which his psyche is disturbed, Razumov comes, by way of his own selfish desire, to seek what is for him the simplest way out, without care or concern for the student who has pinned all his faith on him, to the decision to betray, and temporarily expiates his conscience by the meditation which has already been quoted (page 83). Conrad, having given us this information, prevents us from making any excuses at all for Razumov (should we want to) by telling us that

> He had simply discovered what he had meant to do all along (pp. 38–9).

Despite Conrad's note of censure here, Razumov continues to command our sympathies. He is an unfortunate, and he has been forced into a wretched position. Until his final decision, his loyalties have quite genuinely been pulling him in two opposite directions; and even after his self-discovery he experiences (p. 39) a longing for "a word of advice, for moral support".

This indeed is where Razumov's weakness really lies, in his morality; for his motivation not only comes entirely from self —in his circumstances where else could it possibly come from?—but it takes into account Razumov's self only. In going to the Authorities Razumov is not being loyal to his father so much as running to his father because the situation has got beyond his control—and suiting himself. He is here demonstrating his own moral immaturity in restoring to the natural behaviour of a child when danger threatens. Like a child also, he is unable to see that such an action involves putting himself entirely at the mercy of the aristocratic machine. But whether he realises it at first or not he is now morally implicated whatever he may have been before and in spite of his "malicious pleasure" (p. 50) at Haldin's fate; and Conrad makes the implication of this the more complex by Razumov's secrecy over the Ziemianitch episode, again showing his totally selfish attitude to the whole situation.

> It seemed to him bizarre that secrecy should play such a large part in the comfort and safety of lives. But he wanted to put the Prince's mind at ease; and with a proper amount of emphasis he said that . . . he trusted the future to his own exertions (p. 52).

Despite the naïveté of this and of his father's "You have only to persevere", Razumov is now fettered in a moral situation.

Both father and son seem to overlook the fact that no such experience closes with the abruptness of its opening. That Razumov is forced to realise this simple fact with amazing speed should come as no surprise to us. Even on the walk home, he has to concentrate his reason on familiarity. Already the feeling of strangeness engendered by his new-found moral position is making itself felt.

> The sense of life's continuity depended on trifling bodily impressions. The trivialities of daily existence were an armour for the soul. And this thought reinforced the inward quietness of Razumov as he began to climb the stairs familiar to his feet in the dark, with his hand on the familiar clammy bannister. The exceptional could not prevail against the material contrasts which make one day resemble another. Tomorrow would be like yesterday.
> It was only on the stage that the unusual was outwardly acknowledged (pp. 53–4).

One does not have to read the unnaturally forced reasoning into this. It stands out from every line along with the occasional epithet, such as 'clammy' which brings out Razumov's unnatural awareness of how familiar it all is. He is clearly also refusing to acknowledge the emotional change in himself which is the result of his moral obligation.

This is the true emotional turning point, the commencement of self-awareness, and the beginning of his acknowledgement of his moral commitment. He is no longer, it seems, quite so isolated, at any rate physically. But with that, he has lost his independence, and as for his emotional and moral circumstances, these will have to be discussed later.

As soon as Razumov realises the loss of his security, he longs once more to give vent to his hatred for Haldin to such an extent that it becomes translated into the physical desire to throttle him. His hatred is now more the result of his own guilt at having betrayed Haldin; for this action is marked by no selfless idealism as was Haldin's. Razumov lacked any awareness, let alone any conviction, that he was morally bound to Haldin or to the government by a moral necessity. Had he been, he might have been motivated by it to perform a disinterested action. However, his action is rather more potent than this might make it seem. Instead of acting whole-heartedly on his own, either by throttling Haldin or by genuinely helping, Razumov goes to Ziemianitch and then to the police. In this way he betrays while appearing to assist, an act of outrageous moral cowardice. Here again we see him lacking a true morally positive action either way, and, through sheer failure properly to examine the situation, he compromises himself into a situation where he can be conscripted into becoming a secret agent, also significantly a double job. In tragic terms this is the *Diké* for Razumov's *hubris*.

Despite the fact that it is the working out of this *Diké* that provides the whole of the material for the novel's develop-ment, one should not allow critical comment to blind one to Conrad's manipulation of his material. It is perhaps because Razumov is shown to us as such an unfortunate, such an *ingénu* even, that he never for a moment relaxes the grip he holds on our sympathies. The reader almost automatically identifies himself with the injured Razumov, disturbed in his room, and thus deprived of his heart's ambition. This is per-haps because one is here wholly unconscious of the delayed narrative technique. Conrad, with an acute sense of timing, has allowed the Professor of Languages to sink and merge into the background, and in these pages we come as close to Razumov as we ever come to one of Conrad's creations. The constant repetition of "It's done . . . And now to work . . . It is done" (p. 64), only serves to accentuate the fact that it is really only beginning, and Razumov's autocratic cynicism in-creases as the shock of his contact with Haldin takes effect. As one might expect, this brings to Razumov a more likely awareness of the reality of his situation. Next night he lies in bed in exactly the same position as that adopted by Haldin, and thus symbolises for us his future role as a follower of Haldin into the world of self-torment and victimisation. He sees himself as a suspect and wonders for how long; and, from our point of view much more importantly—for it has a vital bearing on the morality of the situation—he starts trying to exculpate himself for his behaviour towards Haldin. This is his moral condition during his conversations with fellow students, and this is the state of his awareness when the police search his room. The search, however, provides him with the first real kick into an environment where morality matters.

> The feeling that his moral personality was at the mercy of these lawless forces was so strong that he asked himself seriously if it was worth while accomplishing the mental functions of that existence which seemed no longer his own (pp. 77–8).

This is a section of the novel where the confusions of personality which Razumov is facing seem to force him to speak only *double-entendres*, and with unwitting meaning his landlady speaks them back to him:

> "The world is full of black hearts and false denunciations nowadays" (p. 76).

So the full effect of his action comes home to him with a physical directness which merely symbolises the moral consequences.

> The disorder affected him profoundly, unreasonably. He sat down and stared. He had a distinct sensation of his very existence being undermined in some mysterious manner, of his moral supports falling away from him one by one (pp. 76–7).

What he as yet fails to see is that he is himself the destroyer of his moral supports. He has failed his moral test and must take the consequences. When Conrad points out that

> The consequences of their actions were always clear and their lives remained their own (p. 78),

he is indicating first that Razumov's life no longer is his own, and second that the simple reason for this is his failure to think of consequences. He acted through impulse, by impetus, or, more accurately, by a whole series of wavering impetus and also, more significantly, through self-love.

These are, however, not the only forces which combine to compel Razumov. Madcap Kostia's action in offering him money to escape follows the general pattern of the chain of events here. So do the actions of the police and the subtle manipulations of the sinister Councillor Mikulin. He is almost the personification of Razumov's "destructive horror":

> "I want to guide my conduct by reasonable convictions, but what security have I against something—some destructive horror walking in upon me as I sit here?" (p. 78),

except that it is Razumov who walks in to Mikulin's room and not the other way round. Once again we see Razumov desperately trying to command his "cool, superior reason" and at the same time being the initiator and instigator of his own downfall. He finds himself pushed from one side of the political halfpenny to the other. Having been implicated by Haldin in something he wanted nothing at all to do with, he now permits Mikulin to do exactly the same thing from the opposite side; and only in this context does he realise the full, terrifying depth of his implication.

> And it is all over. You cannot shake it off any more. It will cling to you for ever. Neither halter nor bullet can give you back the freedom of your life and the sanity of your thought (p. 84).

Even to him in his realisation, the egocentricity of his outlook still comes naturally and unwittingly to his thoughts. While before Mikulin, he sees that he is in a position of double compromise; and he is entirely responsible for this himself. It is not necessarily of his own volition, but his character, personality and background combine to form the responsibility for the total situation. Understandably "his self-confidence was much shaken" (p. 90) and Razumov goes through the largely self-inflicted, though none the less terrifying, torments of the interview.

> At that moment Razumov beheld his own brain suffering on the rack—a long, pale figure drawn asunder horizontally with terrific force in the darkness of a vault, whose face he failed to see. It was as though he dreamed for an infinitesimal fraction of time of some dark print of the Inquisition (p. 88).

So overpowering is the impression of an inquisition which he derives from this interview that Razumov is on the point of confessing the whole sad business. He sees the whole thing as a macabre "comedy of persecution" (p. 99), and thus we

need to know nothing of his reaction to Mikulin's final enig-
matic "Where to?" (p. 99). This phrase coming as it does
right at the end of Part One is given by Conrad the greatest
strength and power it is technically possible to bestow upon it.
Indeed the whole of this section of *Under Western Eyes* shows
Conrad's keen perception of how to provide a unit of meaning
with additional force either by placing it at the end of a section
or sub-section, or else by allowing the words to form, on their
own, a single short paragraph sandwiched between two
lengthy and verbose paragraphs. In this case, however, the
two interrogatory words "Where to?" not only puzzle the
reader, thus providing a link into the next part of the novel,
but also possess an innate obscurity which mirrors the doubt,
distress and confusion in Razumov's own mind.

(vii)

So we can move from the basic statement of the novel's
situation into the Second Part, where the development of
the moral circumstance for Razumov will be our main concern. It is in fact many pages before Haldin's 'friend' again
features, and when he does so he has himself taken on the
proportions of an enigma "unstained lofty and solitary"
(p. 135). This is the appearance he gives. To the reader who
knows the inner reality, the truth of the man, only the last of
the epithets is acceptable, while we need have no difficulty at
all in fully appreciating the significance of the narrator-
professor's incredible judgement,

"Compromised politically, I suppose" (p. 135).

Indeed there are in these pages several quotations to which
we need to pay special attention. First of all we have restated
for us the background significance in the Russian (Miss
Haldin's) point of view, made to the English Professor.

". . . you hate revolution; you fancy it's not quite honest. You
belong to a people which has made a bargain with fate, and
wouldn't like to be rude to it. But we have made no bargain. It
was never offered to us—so much liberty" (p. 134).

The most interesting thing about this comment is the duplicity of its application. As it is worded, it clearly speaks directly to the Professor. But just as easily, and with just as much truth, it could be applied to Razumov himself. In this way Nathalie unknowingly allies Razumov to her. It puts them in the same camp, as it were, at least as far as race and liberty are concerned. But at the same time, these words make Razumov an outsider. He has, although unwittingly, none the less made his bargain with fate, and at the same time he shares the view of revolutionary activity attributed to the Professor, and thus to the English in general. But when it comes to a direct comment on Razumov, Nathalie can do no better than

> "Only think—such a friend. The only man mentioned in his letters. He would have something to give me, if nothing more than a few poor words. It may be something said and thought in those last days. Would you want me to turn my back on what is left of my poor brother—a friend?" (p. 137).

If anything, Conrad over-exploits the irony of the situation.

> "He seems to be a man who has suffered more from his thoughts than from evil fortune" (p. 168).

Razumov could not be more misunderstood.

> . . . this distressed him. He was quite overcome. I have told you my opinion that he is a man of deep feeling—it is impossible to doubt it. You should have seen his face. He positively reeled. He leaned against the wall of the terrace. Their friendship must have been the very brotherhood of souls! (p. 172).

None of the Russian community in Geneva can understand why Razumov has stayed away from the Haldins, but to us —who know the truth behind the situation—it is obvious. Even the Professor, in many ways such a perceptive character, although able to trace Razumov's resentment when left alone with him, fails to trace its cause. Their relationship naturally is no easy one, for the Professor, in trying to be loyal to his pupil, for whom he feels an acute affection, only aggravates the canker of Razumov's suffering by such remarks as:

> There was something peculiar about the circumstances of his arrest. You, no doubt, know the whole truth (p. 186).

91

So he becomes the more puzzled at his failure to draw Razumov out of himself.

> I said to myself: "He puts on the callousness of a stern revolutionist, the insensibility to common emotions of a man devoted to a destructive idea" (p. 189).

But the Professor is not simply yet another of Razumov's tormentors. He also provides the verbal expression of Razumov's responsibility to the Haldins.

> ". . . but you may believe my assertions that these words are forcible enough to make both his mother and his sister believe implicitly in the worth of your judgement and in the truth of anything you may have to say to them. It's impossible for you now to pass them by like strangers" (p. 190).

And although the narrative method here has altered so that we are no longer so wrapped up in Razumov that we cannot focus on to him disinterestedly, we remain completely sympathetic to him not only because of his voluble outbursts but because all the Professor's judgements go wrong simply because he misunderstands the nature of the relationship between Razumov and Haldin. In letting him persevere in his far from accurate belief that, to Razumov, Haldin appears heroic, Conrad has provided us with a narrator of limited knowledge who retains a moral perspective for the reader, but also allows the hero to retain our sympathies. The key to this section lies in Razumov's "bitterness" at his "wrecked life" and the curse Razumov believes himself to be under, a curse which the Professor mistakenly believes to be the curse of all the Russians.

> "I think that you people are under a curse" (p. 198).

There is no suggestion here that the Professor brings no truth at all to bear on the situation, but when he does so it is usually unwittingly, or only with a half-truth.

> ". . . this extraordinary man is meditating some vast plan, some great undertaking; he is possessed by it—he suffers from it—and from being alone in the world" (p. 202).

It is at this stage in the development of *Under Western Eyes* that Razumov's need of a confidant, and his overwhelming desire to express himself, finally become consummated in his writing of a diary. He sees the "moral suicide" of leaving Geneva, and with a reason which the speaker does not begin to understand, Peter Ivanovitch considers him a "marked personality" (p. 206). Like virtually everyone else in the novel so far, he is voicing the truth about Razumov, but he is doing it unwittingly, and he is therefore unaware of the significance of his analysis. This has been yet another of Razumov's misfortunes right the way through. From the start it seems almost as if his urge to achieve recognition has been the reason why everyone misapprehends his personality. Haldin saw him as a lone conspirator in whom absolute trust could be lodged. Mikulin's interpretation was of a man born for the job of secret agent as if it were his vocation. From our omniscient position as readers, we know the inaccuracy of both views. Initially, Razumov demanded only one thing of life; the right to work alone towards his own intended goal, and this goal was simply that he should be recognised by his own family. But even this entails the sort of selfishness which had characterised his behaviour towards Haldin in the first place.

The Borel group, however, is blind to Razumov's faults of personality. Nor is there any reason why this should be beyond the bounds of reality, for, between them, as I hope has been previously demonstrated, they provide an incredible assortment of undesirable characteristics. Their willingness to accept him as 'one of us' is in marked contrast to Razumov's own immediate reaction which resolves itself into a desire to murder Peter Ivanovitch. The fact that this desire is so strong that Razumov had positively to check himself against it endows it with the same amount of reality as the vision of Haldin which had come over him on the return walk from Ziemianitch. Despite the change of function, and the change in location, this is without a doubt the same Razumov as we sympathised with in the first part of the novel. But if functions and locations have changed, we might do well to ask ourselves what has happened to Razumov's aims, and whether, if there is a change there, the alteration in outlook which this would involve might possibly contribute to a change in personality.

As has just now been suggested, in Part One Razumov was working towards what was essentially a very simple ideal, the acquisition of enough scholarship to ensure him personal recognition. But now scholarship has been entirely ruled out of his life. What substitute is offered him? The only immediate aspect of his character which becomes so patently obvious that it is noticed by all the Borel anarchists, with the exception of the rather more humane and tolerant Tekla, is his 'superiority' and his pride (*v.* p. 209). If we ask ourselves what specific connotations Conrad wishes these words to convey to his readers, we are forced to the conclusion that this is in fact another indication of the self-centredness of Razumov's character. Clearly Conrad does not wish us to see him as 'morally' superior, simply because he is not a revolutionary. To them his superiority consists in the fact that he is solitary, cold and distant to them. In a word, they find him stand-offish. It is the result of his growth in hatred towards all who have deprived him of his university place, aristocrats and anarchists alike.

We can appreciate this fact better if we contrast his 'superiority' towards the majority of the *habitués* of the Château Borel with his attitude to and relationship with the Dame de Compagnie. At first he seems cold and calculating in his approach to her. Having realised once again that he has the 'gift of inspiring confidence', he decides to cultivate her. But the fact that he at the same time wonders what her fellow anarchists have done to her shows that, within the relationship there is, even on Razumov's part, the germ of human interest. This is only another aspect of his lack of family background. He has a deep psychological need to tell, to be understood, and to experience the satisfaction of a relationship with another human being which involves receiving as well as giving. For this is what Razumov has been utterly deprived of; firstly a normal family background, and secondly the right to make demands on other people. Instead, he has merely been the butt of the demands of others. His experiences with both Haldin and Mikulin have taxed him sorely. He has had to yield greatly to both, and has received from neither any reward save that of hardship.

Should one still doubt Razumov's need for a soul-mate, one only has to read how close he comes to a total expression of the truth, when he tells of seeing the phantom of the living person he hated. His words with Peter Ivanovitch, also, reflect this.

"Ah, Peter Ivanovitch, if you only knew the force which drew— no, which *drove* me towards you! The irresistible force" (p. 228).

This, like his confession that he is engaged on secret work of his own, accentuates his feelings of loneliness and betrayal. He sees himself as a pawn that can be moved at the whimsy of either side, and this too throws him back on himself. So it is not surprising that his introspection at last arrives at the morality of his situation, and with admirable self-knowledge at last Razumov comes to doubt the power of his moral resistance. Moral endurance could provide him with his one chance for survival within this situation, and he doubts his own capacity here. This moral resistance, however, cannot be anything other than a facet of his private moral scheme. Razumov must erect a protective barrier in order that his own person can be defended against the two moral schemes of both administrators—the government and anarchists—between whom he is torn. This is an incredibly acute moral problem which Razumov has to face. To him neither public scheme is morally justifiable; both utilise the individual in an indefensible manner. So, Razumov has no alternative. He must produce a scheme of his own that will allow him to survive somewhere between these two. This is his way of life, his hatred and his basic motivation. But it does not take into account the psychological needs of the human being. This is really the common fault of all three schemes. Razumov thinks that because he has been alone in the past and has been betrayed into a totally hostile and inimical situation, he has no need of human company. He does not even realise the extent of his own sympathy towards Tekla, and this provides a sort of forewarning of his love for the far more desirable Nathalie.

A further indication of this aspect of Razumov's character is provided by the example of his relationship with Sophia Antonovna. Or her we learn early that

> he could not despise her as he despised all the others (p. 242).

Our respect for her is increased by her assessment of Razumov, and the directness of her accusation

> "What's the matter with you is that you don't like us" (p. 243).

But still Conrad works upon the irony of the overall situation, by this same technique as we have noticed him using before. When Razumov says

> "I am very much in earnest about my mission" (p. 244),

we know that he means to fulfil his function of secret agent by finding some means of giving vent to his hatred of the anarchists. But more than this, we know that the anarchists will interpret this use of the term 'mission' as meaning the fulfilment of their desire that Nathalie should be persuaded to join their ranks. This continued use of dramatic irony on Razumov's part has two possible interpretations. He may talk down to them in this way because he genuinely feels himself to be superior to them in the way that they have all previously tacitly noticed. In this case, 'superior' would mean 'superior in intelligence' and his use of irony thus becomes merely an outlet for a game which he is playing with them all. But if there is in this anything which can be seen as analogous to the cat-and-mouse situation, then there can be little doubt that it is Razumov who exemplifies the mouse. Hence the more likely interpretation is that this is just another proof of the psychological torment which he is suffering. It is a further expression of his desperate need to share with someone else, and this speaking of half-truths in such a way that they can be interpreted without casting suspicion on him is the nearest he can come to it. This change in personality, if such it amounts to, consists of an outward movement on Razumov's part towards the three women connected with the Château Borel: Tekla, Sophia Antonovna and Nathalie. One should not really need to exempt Mme de S—

here. She is no longer a possible soul-mate for any human being. Even Peter Ivanovitch, it should be remembered, is only loyal to her because he hopes to benefit by her will; and even here, this hope is to be frustrated.

Sophia Antonovna is rather more critical of Razumov than are her colleagues. Indeed, her questioning air is reflected and symbolised by the very angle of her hat. She gets further than the other revolutionaries in her assessment of Razumov, particularly in

"You might think he was one of those nervous sensitives who come to a bad end" (p. 248),

and

"You are feeding on some bitterness of your own" (p. 255),

but beyond this she is as blind as all the rest. None have learned, despite their stated concern for the alleviation of the proletariat, how to release the key-spring of the individual suffering human being. They all seem to realise that Razumov is motivated by bitterness, but none of them for a moment think that this bitterness could be directed against them.

(viii)

This is the state of things which seems to exist for a rather over-long period of the novel, until matters begin to be rushed to a head by the news brought to Sophia Antonovna from Hull, telling her of the death of Ziemianitch. At this point the notion of remorse first enters the pages of *Under Western Eyes*.

"Remorse, indeed! It was a striking example of your true conspirator's blindness, of the stupid subtlety of people with one idea" (p. 283).

It is of course not Razumov who is supposed to have experienced the remorse, but Ziemianitch himself. The Borel group's interpretation is the one that more than adequately covers Razumov, for Ziemianitch is now seen as the betrayer of Haldin, and his death the result of his remorse. What

G
97

makes this all the more crucial to Razumov's predicament is that this alone is a part of the story that he has confessed to no one, not even to his friends in the government. On the surface, Razumov is now utterly safe. The only person who could have exposed him is dead. But emotionally he is in a worse situation than ever. His power of moral endurance is clearly to be taxed to the full, and, as we know, his one outlet for this is provided by the self-expression of his diary, a writing-up for himself of his own confessions.

> "Extraordinary occupation I am giving myself up to," he muttered. And it occurred to him that this was the only sound he could listen to innocently, and for his own pleasure, as it were. Yes, the sound of water, the voice of the wind—completely foreign to human passions. All the other sounds of this earth brought contamination to the solitude of a soul (p. 291).

Conrad seems anxious to fuse together in Razumov's sensibility the whole situation, the whole location of where he writes his diary—the island ironically decorated with funeral urns—with the actual performance of writing the diary. Thus place and action together provide the only moments of relief that his life contains. This doubtless explains why

> the bitterness of solitude from which he suffered was not an altogether morbid phenomenon (p. 292).

This is virtually how we find Razumov near the beginning of Part Four of *Under Western Eyes*.

> "Perhaps life is just that," reflected Razumov, pacing to and fro under the trees of the little island all alone with the bronze statue of Rousseau. "A dream and a fear" (p. 316).

This does not, however, mean that Razumov has come to any closer grips with his situation, or that he is more confident of his power to survive. Now more than ever he is conscious of Haldin's death.

> It was impossible to get rid of him. "It's myself whom I have given up to destruction," thought Razumov. "He has induced me to do it. I can't shake him off" (p. 341).

This does not, however, stop him from trying to extricate himself from the society of others by seeking refuge on the Rousseau island. Indeed this becomes almost symbolic for his survival. Conrad has almost allowed his isolation theme to suffer an inversion. Razumov desires solitude. He wants to be alone, and no one will let him. As has been suggested, Razumov's greatest need is as yet supplied by his diary, which "calmed him—it reconciled him to his existence" (p. 339). This reconciliation is necessitated by the moral situation which Razumov has at last come to realise. He now sees that those actions which he believed to be right for himself personally were in fact the opposite. They have begun a landslide of events which has brought about the destruction of his moral being. In the context of public morality—that is the moral code adopted as right by the authorities of the state—his actions can be interpreted as right ones. This does not, however, answer the problem of whose moral scheme was the right one. Should Razumov have supported Haldin entirely; or should he have gone to the police in the first instance? If we are here expecting Conrad to tell us whether, in matters of public morality, the individual has a right to question the ins and outs of a situation without just following, say, the political leaders blindly, we are forced to accept the example Razumov gives us. The issue arising out of the public scheme of morality only becomes really important when the individual's private morality is an adequate one. So, finally, he has to come to grips with the physical embodiment of his nightmare, Haldin's sister, and the actual existence of any relationship at all provides him with something like relief.

> He had such a strong sense of Natalia Haldin's presence that to look at her he felt would be a relief. It was she who had been haunting him now. He had suffered that persecution ever since she had suddenly appeared before him in the garden of the Villa Borel with an extended hand and the name of her brother on her lips (p. 342).

But whereas with the anarchists Razumov has been able to view them with such a degree of ironic disinterestedness that his survival has had even chances, the positive contact with

Haldin's family has an acute ethos about it which compels him to be more aware than ever of the immorality of his behaviour. He, the cause of the son's death, finds himself the comforter of the bereaved mother. Nathalie, too, early begins to doubt the completeness of Razumov's relationship with Haldin,

> "It seems as if you were keeping back something from me" (p. 351).

This and the news about Ziemianitch show the dawning of a new consciousness which combines with Razumov's need to communicate and his growing affection for Nathalie to produce the following conversation.

> "Tell me, Nathalia Victorovna, . . . do you believe in remorse?"
> "What a question!"
> "What can *you* know of it?" he muttered thickly. "It is not for such as you . . . What I meant to ask was whether you believed in the efficacy of remorse?"
> She hesitated as though she had not understood, then her face lighted up.
> "Yes," she said firmly.
> "So he is absolved . . ." (p. 352).

He trusts and respects Nathalie's opinion, and yet feels himself the need for absolution. He is in fact now feeling remorse himself. He is at the beginning of that sequence of reasoning which will impel him to go to Nathalie with his confession. For the moment, however, he can find no release from his remorse. Quite simply, he has no one to go to and she "was unable to see the truth struggling on his lips" (p. 354). We too are caught unawares. Though knowing that it is bound to come, it is not at once obvious that his confession is here and now. And after it, in the melancholy of sheer love, he picks up the veil that she had dropped.

As Razumov walks home through the thunderstorm he feels that he is "washed clean" (p. 357), absolutely purged. Physically and symbolically the storm also purges him. His diary, we now learn, is not just a piece of whimsical self-confession. All along it has been addressed to Nathalie. She has been his chosen confidant from the time when he first began to write. And he sees himself, in his self-pity, as being successful in "stealing her soul from her" (p. 359), as his own, he believed, had been stolen from him. Despite the "might of falsehood" (p. 360) between them and despite the force of his hatred, he had "ended by loving her" (p. 360), and has studied her so closely in his longing that he can now recall every physical detail of her appearance. He has at last come to the only true conclusion about his actions:

> "in giving Victor Haldin up, it was myself, after all, whom I have betrayed most basely" (p. 361).

With these thoughts he comes to his final confession. He is unable now to shirk the rectifying of his mistaken morality.

> He was the puppet of his past, because at the very stroke of midnight he jumped up and ran swiftly downstairs as if confident that, by the power of destiny, the house door would fly open before the absolute necessity of his errand. And as a matter of fact, just as he got to the bottom of the stairs, it was opened for him . . . (p. 362).

Everything is in his favour now for him to absolve himself. But absolution is never easy, and although he has come to the point where morality has become simple and straightforward to understand, if not so easy to perform, Conrad reminds us that this is still the same Razumov. His speech to the conspirators is marked by the independence and pride of Razumov's former self.

> "I beg you to observe," he said, already on the landing, "that I had only to hold my tongue. Today, of all days since I came amongst you, I was made safe, and today I made myself free from falsehood, from remorse—independent of every single human being on this earth" (p. 368).

This is what is really important to him, a free spirit. His remorse can no longer trouble him. His physical disabilities are irrelevant to the spiritual torture he has suffered since almost the beginning of the novel. Deaf and crippled by a tram he could not hear, he is cared for by Tekla. This in itself still contains an illusion. All the time, Tekla has lamented her shattered illusions, and yet, as a true anarchist, she performs her idealistic duty in nursing the anti-anarchist. The fact that she still understands him to be the slayer of M. de P—, and the colleague, not the betrayer, of Victor Haldin, is not important. Her life has found a meaning in caring for Razumov's last months of unregretted independence.

(ix)

The last word on the whole episode is really Nathalie's. It should be remembered that she had been the recipient of Razumov's diary, wrapped up in her returned veil, and her words are really the conclusion to Razumov's story.

"But at last the anguish of hearts shall be extinguished in love" (p. 377).

So those who are left as the principal characters at the end of the novel, Nathalie and Tekla, are left devoted to the cause of love. And Razumov? His life too has refound its meaning. His love may have defeated him in the physical sense that he is maimed and will soon die. But he has re-achieved self-esteem. He has also been recognised for the truth of what he is, and can die at least spiritually content. After the confession Sophia Antonovna at least can offer the Professor of Languages an adequate comment on the morality of the whole affair.

"There are evil moments in every life. A false suggestion enters one's brain, and then fear is born—fear of oneself, fear for oneself. Or else a false courage—who knows? Well, call it what you like; but tell me, how many of them would deliver themselves up deliberately to perdition (as he himself says in that book) rather than go on living, secretly debased in their own eyes? How many? . . . And please mark this—he was safe when he did it. It was just when he believed himself safe and more—infinitely more—when the possibility of being loved by that admirable girl first dawned upon him, that he discovered that his bitterest railings, the worst wickedness, the devil work of his hate and pride, could never cover up the ignominy of the existence before him. There's character in such a discovery" (pp. 379–80).

This is the reasoning behind the forgiveness and compassion of the only other anarchist to gain Razumov's respect.

And that is how Razumov lives on. The detailed treatment here of the personal moralities involved, it should perhaps be stressed again, is not meant to suggest that the novel contains nothing more than this, no national or political over- and under-tones, for example. One need only refer to the following paragraph to see that the Professor, for example, is very much alive to the possibilities of love and common nationalistic feelings.

> In fact, I thought the Bastions a very convenient place since the girl did not think it prudent as yet to introduce that young man to her mother. It was here, then, I thought, looking round at that plot of ground of deplorable banality, that their acquaintance will begin and go on in the exchange of generous indignations and of extreme sentiments, too poignant, perhaps, for a non-Russian mind to conceive. I saw these two, escaped out of four score of millions of human beings ground between the upper and nether millstone, walking under these trees, their young heads close together. Yes, an excellent place to stroll and talk in. It even occurred to me, while we turned once more away from the wide iron gates, that when tired they would have plenty of accommodation to rest themselves. There was a quantity of tables and chairs displayed between the restaurant chalet and the bandstand, a whole raft of painted deals spread out under the trees. In the very middle of it I observed a solitary Swiss couple, whose fate was made secure from the cradle to the grave by the perfected mechanism of democratic institutions in a republic that could almost be held in the palm of one's hand. The man, colourlessly uncouth, was drinking beer out of a glittering glass; the woman, rustic and placid, leaning back in the rough chair, gazed idly around (p. 175).

But the main arena of the novel, at least as far as this particular study is concerned, is a psychological and moral one, for it shows the interweavings and complementations of psychology and morality. Morality is shown here as being as complex as the individual's psychology. This goes some of the way towards explaining why there are, in *Under Western Eyes*, so many different attitudes towards Razumov, as well as interpretations of his behaviour. The morality of Haldin's bomb-throwing, for example, provides us with a good instance of the complexity of all these different schemata. To the Authorities, including of course Prince K—, he is a villain and therefore worthy of execution, no matter how he comes into their hands. Nathalie, his sister, however, is at first at a loss to know what to think, and the question of her attitude towards the initial assassination is at first shelved by her acceptance of the grief which comes with the news of her brother's death. It is only by the implications of her conduct at the end of the novel, and beyond its end, that we can see that her attitude towards the alleviation of an unhappy lot is a positive one. She goes out to help the suffering. To take the negative attitude of destroying by destruction, as her brother had done, is clearly no real answer. To Ivanovitch, at least in his anarchical pose, Haldin is a hero and a martyr, while to Razumov himself he seems selfish and inconsiderate, amoral in the sense of the private scheme of morality. But one must remember all the time that the interpretation of the morality of any given action depends also on the morality of the interpreter. Only the novelist and his reader, viewing from a world outside fiction, can achieve such a degree of disinterested participation as to be able to pass complete moral judgements on the characters of the novel. This is the real achievement of *Under Western Eyes*, for it is only in this way that Razumov can be seen as a hero. There is a multiplicity of experience in the novel which allows that, just as in real life, no two people will predictably act in the same way. Thus, though all the characters trust Razumov, they trust him for different reasons. For example, Nathalie's acceptance of him stems from the mention of him in her brother's letters, while Tekla's derives from the fact that he treated her as an equal human being, symbolised for us by his action of raising his hat to her. But the point really is that Conrad achieves a situation in which all his characters accept Razumov without straining the bounds of possibility. In just the same way, though each character and, in this case, each reader has his own different moral views, the final judgement on Razumov will remain the same. His redemption has been achieved. He has been able to win back his self-esteem and, whatever the physical loss involved, has won for himself moral wholeness.

4

'Nostromo'

NOSTROMO is, at one and the same time, the story of
a mine, a community and of one individual, but so finely
is the narrative blended that the reader is in no sense aware
of the novel having separate plots or sub-plots. Nostromo—
the individual—is the Italian Capataz of the local Cargadores
employed by the Oceanic Steam Navigation Company, at
their depot at Costaguana, the scene of the novel as a whole.
Here also is the Gould Concession, a hitherto unworkable
silver mine, heavily taxed by the government. In the novel,
however, Charles and Emily Gould, who have inherited the
mine, determine to make it a success in order to relieve
the oppressed population of Costaguana. But this is South
America and every political pretender also has an eye on the
wealth of the Gould Concession for his own ends.

The actual political intrigues need not concern us deeply
as *Nostromo* is not first and foremost a 'political novel' in the
sense of a 'novel about politics' (*v.* Wilding, 'The Politics of
Nostromo', in *Essays in Criticism*, XVI₄, October 1966). All
one needs to remember is that it is through fear of its misuse
in politics that Gould arranges for the worked silver to be
slipped out of Costaguana by lighter with the intention of its
intercepting the O.S.N. steamer which can then transport it
to safety in the United States. However, this is not what
happens, for the silver is hidden on one of the islands in the
gulf, and the lighter is then sunk.

Predictably, Nostromo is one of the two men to whom the
silver is entrusted. The other is Martin Decoud—the darling
of the Paris boulevards—who has been operating a political
newspaper in Sulaco where the Goulds live, and whose life
is consequently forfeit. But Conrad shows us clearly that
Decoud is motivated not by political ideals at all really, but
by love for Antonia Avellanos, a Costaguaneran; and his

virtual hypocrisy may have a lot to do with his death. For, left alone on the island with only the silver for company, he soon commits suicide by drowning, using two of the bars of silver to weight him down.

Nostromo's position is not at all like this. For the first time in his life he has been compelled to act under cover of darkness, literally and metaphorically. Deprived of the public glory on which he has in the past relied, he is overwhelmed by desire for a substitute reward, and he steals the silver simply by pretending that, when the lighter was sunk, the silver was still on board.

With typical irony, Conrad ends the novel with the safety of Sulaco being ensured by Separation, and, since the miners provided the fighting force which protected Gould from execution, the mine itself is also saved, despite the disappearance of so much silver. Nostromo dies returning to visit his adored silver. He has grown rich slowly, and now styles himself Captain Fidanza. But his change of name in no way symbolises a change of character. He has become betrothed to one of the Viola girls, while constantly declaring his love to the other, and he is ultimately shot in error by the father, old Giorgio Viola himself, now the lighthouse-keeper of the island where the silver lies hidden, though introduced earlier in the novel as a café proprietor and a staunch Garibaldino.

This gives the bare outline of the plot, but it is impossible to go on to the discussion of the novel without first mentioning two further characters. Captain Mitchell—the O.S.N. representative—stands in this novel as the staunch, unimaginative, vaguely amusing sea-dog of some of Conrad's other writings. But he also has those qualities which convinced Conrad of the value of the British Merchant Service. He is unimaginative enough not to realise his own danger, when he is in one, and yet courageous enough to defy the most unscrupulous of terrorists. And this range of attributes makes him ideal to be chosen as narrator when Conrad wishes us to gain narrative information from within the novel, rather than omniscient comment from outside.

Dr Monygham also ought to be mentioned at this stage because one needs to realise his background if one is to appreciate his moral force in *Nostromo*, particularly with regard to his relationship with Emily Gould. Monygham appears to everyone who does not know him intimately—and few do—as twisted and embittered. The warping in him seems mental as well as physical. Indeed, Conrad is anxious to show us that his bitterness and his deformity are aspects of each other. For in a previous political *coup*, an event which in historical terms occurred before the beginning of *Nostromo*, Monygham fell to the mercy of the tyrannical Guzman Bento who loosed his chief torturer on the doctor. This is the explanation of why the doctor is crippled, and in itself might have justified Monygham's attitude of mind but, as we shall see, such a self-centred explanation would not suit Conrad's purpose at all well here. Monygham's disillusionment is directed against himself. He is embittered by feelings of guilt and shame which arise from his having invented political lies in order that the torture should be ended. But here again Conrad forces us to sympathise with the doctor. He was not released even after his confession, but kept in total darkness until the fall of the Bento regime.

It is impossible in a précis such as this to do justice to the novel, but one can at least see that, in writing *Nostromo*, Conrad has chosen an altogether larger canvas than in either of the two other novels discussed in this book. This does not just mean that he is dealing with a more ambitious environment, or with far more major personalities. In terms of the moral perspectives the novel embraces, Conrad has opened up into a far wider field. Here, as before, he indicates that morality is two-edged in its implications, it has both a positive ✷ and a negative side. Furthermore, Conrad can use something he disapproves of to symbolise by implication his approval of ✷ its opposite. If then we accept for the moment that one of the chief things that Conrad is writing about in *Nostromo* is material interests, we can at once realise why the silver of the San Tomé mine does not just supply the centre around which the plot revolves. It is also the focus for the moral patterns in the novel. At the time of the first troubles, we learn

Most of the Europeans in Sulaco were there, rallied round Charles Gould, as if the silver of the mine had been the emblem of a common cause, the symbol of the supreme importance of material interests (p. 260).

Conrad is here once again using the ironic mode to show his disapproval of such an obsession with material interests; what he is really concerned with are the different types of moral behaviour which arise out of contact with such material interests as these. At another point in the novel, he voices clearly the moral concern that he holds to be so overridingly important.

The mine had been the cause of an absurd moral disaster; its working must be made a serious and moral success (p. 66).

This is Conrad's plain statement of the relationship between morality and material interests. It is the signpost of what the novel is all about. Material interests have debased morality, they have caused a moral pollution. The mine can only be redeemed by a right-minded morality; only morality can justify the material interests involved.

Our purpose therefore is to trace the moral patterns that surround the material interests of the San Tomé mine in terms of the conduct and attitudes of the characters who appear in *Nostromo*. For the sake of convenience, these characters can be classified into four groups. Firstly, there is Gould himself, the owner of the mine, in whom, as in his father, there occurs an obsession, and for whom the mine becomes an end in itself, and not a means to a far greater end. Secondly, there are those characters like Holroyd, Montero, Sotillo and Hirsch, before his cowardice completely takes over. These also express, in their actions and their motives, a concern for the welfare of material interests, rather than the care of people. This attitude contrasts directly with that of our third group. This consists of such characters as Don José Avellanos and, of course, Mrs Gould, both of whom show great concern for the public and spiritual welfare of the Costaguaneros and later the Sulacans, and long further to subordinate the silver of the mine to this purpose. In other words, their view is that the mine should be of direct benefit to the people who live near it or even work in it; and we can translate this into a general moral precept by saying that one can only justify material interests morally if they are put to the direct service and betterment of the community, or of society at large. Finally, we come to the personalities of Nostromo and Decoud. For both of these, the silver reflects the turning of natural resources, which by right belong to the community at large, into wholly private and personal gains. I am not claiming here that Nostromo and Decoud are motivated in exactly the same way. The type of private use to which the two of them put the mine is completely different. Indeed, each sees the mine in a totally different light, as I shall hope to show in due course. None the less, it will be advantageous to our discussion to group them together, not just because of the similarity of their downfalls, but because they are motivated in similar ways.

In *Nostromo*, as in *The Secret Agent* and *Under Western Eyes*, Conrad makes specific references in his Author's Note so as to ensure that we are aware of what he is doing and of what he holds most important in the novel. Throughout *Nostromo* our reading is beset by two difficulties—finding out where we are in the chronological sequence of events, and keeping in true perspective the intermingling moral patterns which the characters represent. To help us to find a single moral positive in the midst of all this flux, in other words to provide us with a moral anchor, Conrad writes with very real affection in his Author's Note of "my venerated friend" Don José Avellanos, and his "Fifty Years of Misrule". Don José is not a narrator, but he performs in *Nostromo* the moral function that the Professor of Languages performed in *Under Western Eyes*. He is the norm, as it were. His occasional appearances in the novel are relayed with a sympathy of expression which is absent even from the treatment of Antonia or Mrs Gould. So when we are confused as to what is good and what is bad, when we are unable to make moral judgements on the motives of Conrad's characters in this novel, we can turn to Don José knowing that he represents the entirely good, especially in his concern for his fellow creatures. His actions may not always come out in the right way—this is one of the difficulties between the two concepts of what we believe may be the right course of action, and what ultimately turns out to have been the right one, a distinction which was discussed in the last chapter—but he always acts from the best possible motives. Once we have realised this, we can easily move to the next stage. This is when we see that Mrs Gould, again simply because she is concerned for people, is also a character whose temperament and wishes are to be approved with few reservations.

(i)

It is no use pretending that *Nostromo* is an easy book to read, particularly when one is coming to it for the first time. One of the crucial difficulties arises out of its title. Whenever the Capataz de Cargadores enters the novel's sphere of action we tend to pay him a lot of attention simply because we have been conditioned by the title to expect a lot of him. A reader might well ask himself whether in fact this expectation is justifiable. Clearly we are concerned more with the individual characters and the way in which they group themselves together by their moral outlooks than with the separation of Sulaco from Costaguana. Thus Mitchell's account of the thriving Occidental Republic to the distinguished but bored and confused visitor of the O.S.N. is, in a sense, the conclusion of the story. But Conrad inserts it some hundred pages before the book's conclusion. This has the technical advantage of leaving the arena clear for the true climax of the novel *qua* work of art. Now this climax, that is the artistic climax, belongs to Nostromo and the world of personal values and the conduct of the individual. All of this is specifically opposed to any public implications Conrad's moralities may contain. However, although the actual end of the book, in terms of pages, belongs to Nostromo, there are plenty of other characters just as central to its morality. Decoud at once comes to mind. He does the right things, as we shall see, but, like Nostromo himself, he does them for the wrong reasons. All the time he seems to us to be distant. Only at his death, where his morality no longer matters, do we come at all close to him, for he is no longer the Decoud of the earlier pages, but a lone man in exile unable to face himself, and the creed of moral belief he has set up for himself. His death may temporarily affect us as much as the illness of Don José Avellanos, or the loneliness of Mrs Gould, but this does not ultimately reconcile us to him any the more in personal terms.

The one character who seems to be on both sides, who seems to care for others, and yet to be entirely selfish, is the one it is easiest to misunderstand. Together with Decoud and Nostromo, Dr Monygham makes up the triumvirate of important moral agents in *Nostromo*. One cannot hope, however, to understand either his disposition or his bitterness without first examining his character or his past. It is not until the third part of the book that we begin to find any real evidence that would help us to understand the bitterness of the deformed doctor. Conrad purposely leaves his explanation until late in the book when the realisation that the doctor's cynicism and contempt for his fellow creatures is in fact not callousness, but rather the very lack of it.

> People believed him scornful and soured. The truth of his nature consisted in his capacity for passion and in the sensitiveness of his temperament. What he lacked was the polished callousness of men of the world, the callousness from which springs an easy tolerance for oneself and others; the tolerance wide as poles asunder from true sympathy and human compassion. This want of callousness accounted for his sardonic turn of mind and his biting speeches (p. 520).

It is not, however, by such an analysis as this that Conrad forces us into sympathy with Monygham. Rather he achieves it in the account of the doctor's suffering at the hands of Father Beron, Guzman Bento's interrogator. Monygham had been a difficult victim. So his torture had been the longer and the more acute, and the shame and contempt he felt for himself for having confessed in the end has prevented him from any longer looking anyone in the face. Conrad's account of Monygham's liberation is similarly vivid; his wretched attempts to walk link in our own imaginations with the blinding effect on his eyes of the light of a solitary candle. It is this past suffering which has conditioned his aspect, physically in the weakness of his ankles, and spiritually in the sense of moral degradation he suffers. This moral degradation is a figment of his own self-accusation, but Monygham feels this the more acutely because of the fluency with which he invented imaginary things to confess when he could at last no longer face the torturer. Because he gave full details of a non-existent conspiracy in order that his own suffering might be limited, he despises himself utterly. This is what makes him appear the misanthrope he does. But from all these past experiences stems also his moral outlook. However this morality is also one which is only apparent to the other characters of the novel in a very limited way, partly because it is so conditioned by the doctor's past. Despite his bitterness, he is an idealist. Indeed, the bitterness stems from the idealism, for without it Monygham would never have judged himself so harshly in the first instance. This idealism, as I hope shortly to show, finally becomes focussed into an unwavering personal loyalty to Mrs Gould. His adoration of her is really only an individual aspect of the interest he feels in people generally, but because she clearly manifests the same feeling, Monygham becomes the more acutely aware of her.

> "She thinks of that girl," he said to himself; "she thinks of the Viola children; she thinks of me; of the wounded; of the miners; she always thinks of everybody who is poor and miserable! But what will she do if Charles gets the worst of it in this infernal scrimmage those confounded Avellanos have drawn him into? No one seems to be thinking of her" (p. 380).

His concern, however, as I have just suggested above, is not so selfish as to rest only on her. Because he is concerned for her world, he goes so far as to care for Charles's safety and thus overlooks the fact that Charles, as the husband of the woman the doctor loves, is in every sense his rival. In this way Monygham's spiritual and moral character, hidden under the twistings and bitterness of his worn-out body, transcends the body's limitations.

> The doctor's soul, withered and shrunk by the shame of a moral disgrace, became implacable in the expression of its tenderness (p. 431).

Despite his concentration on the Gould's welfare, Monygham's spiritual self, however, is still in a delicate position. This is shown in his conversation with Nostromo to which reference will shortly have to be made again, where Monygham becomes understandably tetchy and hurt by Nostromo's distrust of his motives. We know, however, that the doctor's motives are entirely selfless, and so he gains the reward of friendship from that very quarter from which he will value it most.

> Mrs Gould shuddered a little at the allusion to the destruction that had come so near to the San Tomé mine.
> "Ah, but you, dear friend?"
> "I did the work I was fit for."
> "You faced the most cruel danger of all. Something more than death."
> "No, Mrs Gould! Only death—by hanging. And I am rewarded beyond my deserts" (p. 507).

If we are to do Monygham full justice as a character, there are two things we must notice in this quotation, beyond the actual statement of the friendship between the two. The first is Monygham's modesty, his self-effacement. He still feels that any death is too good for him, any sacrifice too noble, simply because he gave in to torture so long ago. The second is just as significant. Monygham's success as a person is spiritual. This is what success in terms of personality means. In terms of character, physical success is meaningless. So Monygham is rewarded in wholly spiritual terms, that is by friendship, a deep and meaningful friendship with another man's wife. And it is because there is no physical basis to their relationship that Monygham's reward is so great.

By all this, Conrad, as well as arousing in us sympathy for his suffering under Bento, shows us Monygham as an important moral agent in the novel. His conversation with Nostromo in the Custom House is one of the two most important exchanges in the whole novel as far as the exposition of a morality is concerned. Similarly his interpretation of Nostromo is what ultimately brings us to an understanding of the latter's character. But Monygham is far from being merely a catalyst to our understanding of the Capataz, or a pivot against which we can assess the Goulds. His own moral outlook is simple and important, and it is because of its simplicity that I have been dealing with it first. All Monygham's actions stem from love. At its most personal level, this love engenders in the doctor a total understanding of and sympathy for Mrs Gould. But, as I have suggested above, his understanding and sympathy do not rest on one person alone. As well as Mrs Gould, he understands, for example, Sotillo. Because of this, he can manipulate the latter so that he may serve the former. This the doctor finds the easier to do because, although Mrs Gould may return his understanding, Sotillo is too afraid of Pedrito Montero and— like Charles Gould himself—too obsessed with the idea of the silver, ever to question Monygham's motives. The real difference between the two is that Monygham, by the very nature of his past, has developed a moral sense; Sotillo has none.

> Even in a man utterly devoid of moral sense there remains an appreciation of rascality which, being conventional, is perfectly clear. Sotillo thought that Dr Monygham, so different from all Europeans, was ready to sell his countrymen and Charles Gould, his employer, for some share of the San Tomé silver. Sotillo did not despise him for that. The colonel's want of moral sense was of a profound and innocent character. It bordered upon stupidity, moral stupidity. Nothing that served his ends could appear to him really reprehensible. Nevertheless, he despised Dr Monygham. He had for him an immense and satisfactory contempt. He despised him with all his heart because he did not mean to let the doctor have any reward at all. He despised him, not as a man without faith and honour, but as a fool. Dr Monygham's insight into his character had deceived Sotillo completely. Therefore he thought the doctor a fool (p. 350).

But Monygham is no fool, and all Sotillo's judgements become directed against himself. For the doctor has not been acting for his own ends at all. None the less, his moral sense is of a far from innocent character here. For he is now acting purely for the good of Mrs Gould, and the good of Mrs Gould means the welfare of both her husband, and the San Tomé mine. So the doctor, having become a South American "Machiavelli of Goodness" does everything in his power, even so far as to surrender his life, should the need arise, in order that these ends may be achieved.

A rule of conduct resting mainly on severe rejections is necessarily simple. Dr Monygham's view of what it behoved him to do was severe; it was an ideal view, in so much that it was the imaginative exaggeration of a correct feeling (p. 375).

Motivated in this way, he goes to simulate his game of betrayal to Sotillo, and to prevent him from entering the town. He is not doing what is evil in taking upon himself the part of the liar. He is only appearing to act evilly; and it is those, like Captain Mitchell, who lack imagination or insight, or both, who rebuke him. His "task of love and devotion" makes him play himself into Sotillo's hands, and, for the sake of others, he faces the possibility of a second treatment such as that he suffered at the hands of Beron. There is also, doubtless, some attempt at self-justification in his action, a desire to try, perhaps, to redeem himself in his own eyes. But despite all this, he hates the apparent immorality of his pretended betrayal of the mine to Sotillo. For this reason, Monygham cannot help wishing that he might have been spared this second humiliation and degradation, and that the silver of the mine had been used to buy Sotillo off the town. Like Mrs Gould, Monygham rates the silver as the least important aspect of those things which he cares about. Again like her, he shows a conscious concern most of all for what is happening to the human beings involved. He who, although completely innocent, had suffered probably as much as any human being could suffer, is spurred on to action by the thought of saving others from suffering.

"I don't know," burst out the exasperated doctor. "There are innocent people in danger whose little finger is worth more than you or I and all the Ribierists together" (p. 456).

Monygham's position is the more important simply because of his concern for others. As we shall see, Nostromo and Decoud appear to be acting for the public good. In reality they are acting solely for private ends and for selfish gain.

Monygham is quite the reverse of these. He lets the good action appear bad. So Nostromo's interpretation of his mission to Sotillo is also entirely wrong.

> He understood well that the doctor was anxious to save the San Tomé mine from annihilation. He would be nothing without it. It was his interest (p. 455).

But Nostromo's comment is coloured by the knowledge of what his own action would have been were he in the same circumstances as Monygham. As we now can see, the truth of the matter was very different from its appearance. Monygham, in total self-denial, was not afraid that, by appearing to betray Gould and act immorally, he would gain only the censure of other men and thus be ostracised entirely. Chiefly because of his past, he was unconcerned by what men might think of him. What he did care about was their welfare. So he is an important moral agent in that he stands for what is good. He represents in the novel what is positive in morality. This is why, nearly at the end of the novel, he is present with Mrs Gould and Giselle at Nostromo's death. These are the three who care for people simply because they are people, and accept them still, though knowing their vices as well as their virtues.

(ii)

Decoud is the next character to be discussed. It has already been suggested that he is as central to the moral structure of the plot as is Nostromo himself, if not more so. But his moral position, as I shall hope to show, is quite dissimilar to Monygham's, since his apparently moral actions are the result, very often, of selfish motives, and therefore take on the aura of immorality. Now despite the immorality of his orientation, we are allowed to come closer to Martin Decoud than to anyone else in the novel because of Conrad's use of a first-person narrative, plausibly inserted as a letter to a favourite sister. It is in fact this same letter which provides the second of the crucial exchanges which are the keys to the working out of the novel's morality. It is similarly significant that whereas Monygham's exchange was a two-sided conversation, Decoud's, being a letter to which there is no reply, is one-sided and predominantly selfish. It is a further tribute to Conrad's technique that, despite the closeness to which we can approach Decoud, the narration of his moral position is such that he fails to arouse as much sympathy in us as does Monygham. Our approval of characters in this, as in any other novel, or indeed in real life, depends on their behaving in a way that we can admire. Nowadays, the continuing popularity of Ian Fleming's writings suggest that admiration for a fictional hero stems from an identification between the reader and 007. But by and large, most readers accept that once out of the fantasy world, such behaviour as his just will not do. What really makes us admire any person, fictional or real, is his possession of certain virtues, and the very use of the word virtues here presupposes that the whole question is really a moral one. We laud a character who acts morally; we censure one who does not, though we may have real sympathies for both. Thus we can see that, in *Nostromo*, it is not the first-person mode of narration which makes us applaud, and perhaps occasionally identify ourselves with, a certain character. It may help us to sympathise with a character, as it does with Decoud, whom none the less we must ultimately censure. Conversely, we may feel warm approval for such a character as Mrs Gould, whom we barely know as a person. In fact we know more about Mrs Gould from our study of Monygham and of the personal link between them, than we do from her actual character. It is this approval of character, which is bound to influence our reading of any fiction of merit, which causes the rather complex attitude we have towards Decoud. We are moved by his death in the way already described, but this does not reconcile us any the more towards his life. It is essential to Conrad's moral schemata in *Nostromo* that Decoud should suffer some sort of collapse, but ultimately we must reject him. However much we feel for him and for his death, we know that a dangerous moral influence has been removed, and our long-lasting sympathies will be for the live Antonia rather than the dead Decoud. Nor is our sympathy in any case a contradiction of the moral

117

schema which rejects Decoud. He is an unfortunate. As such we may pity him. But this does not make him any the more moral, and so his death becomes the more meaningful in the terms of the novel as a whole.

We are first introduced to Decoud as an "idle boulevardier" who "was in danger of remaining a sort of nondescript dilettante all his life" (p. 153). He is spared this by his voluntary migration from Paris to Sulaco. In fact he is a native Costaguanero, and only "the adopted child of Western Europe" (p. 156), who uses the pretext of a godfather's request as an opportunity for renewing his acquaintance with this same godfather's daughter, Antonia Avellanos. There is clearly duplicity of purpose already to be seen here. None the less, this combination of compulsive forces, his friendship with Don José, and his adoration for Antonia, which makes him stay in Sulaco after he has completed his gun-running mission, helps to raise him a little in our eyes. So he becomes the journalist of Sulaco, editing the *Porvenir* through which he was able to "voice the aspirations of the province" (p. 158). But we cannot be blind to the fact that his position is a false one, his journalism merely a pretext for continuing his wooing of Antonia. In the safety of Sulaco, he adopts the persona of the militant journalist using the power of the press to further the rights of his countrymen. But it is only a persona, and nothing more.

> He had pushed the habit of universal raillery to a point where it blinded him to the genuine impulses of his own nature (p. 153),

and this is why he has become a man who has lost the power to understand himself. This is, of course, the initial cause of his loss of faith and his suicide. But it all has to be worked out, and Decoud has first to realise the falsehood of his position.

The easiest place for us to see this is in Conrad's account of the tea party at the Casa Gould, in Chapter V of the Second Part, when

> Martin Decoud was angry with himself. All he saw and heard going on around him exasperated the preconceived views of his European civilization. To contemplate revolutions from the

distance of the Parisian Boulevards was quite another matter. Here on the spot it was not possible to dismiss their tragic comedy with the expression, "*Quelle farce!*" (p. 176).

He is entirely out of his element, not just in the environment of the Gould's sitting-room, but in the whole revolutionary atmosphere of South America. But the hollowness of his anti-Montero cries do not deceive him as to the falsehood of his position. He knows that he is writing 'deadly nonsense' where the 'deadly' means that it could well prove fatal to him. And he knows too that it is 'deadly' also in the sense that it is killing his self-respect. So, although his self-respect has by now virtually gone, his knowledge of its having gone allows him to keep his own personal situation in some sort of perspective.

"There is nothing I would not do for the sake of Antonia. There is nothing I am not prepared to undertake. There is no risk I am not ready to run" (p. 213).

There is no lover's hypocrisy in this statement. It has, on the surface, the same ring of sacrifice about it as has much of Monygham's speech. What makes it so different from Monygham's is that it is spoken in the hope of ultimately gaining a positive reward in the hand of Antonia Avellanos. Monygham acted believing any sort of personal reward impossible.

The whole of the tête-à-tête between Martin Decoud and Antonia on the balcony of the Casa Gould is full of deep moral import. Conrad further uses this importance as a foil to override its impropriety according to the customs and the morals of the natives. But the simple fact that he refers to this native code is not without its significance either. In stating his moral outlook to Antonia, Decoud is flouting one set of values for the sake of another. He is behaving here solely for his private self, and thus ignoring both public customs and, along with them, those public ideals and political aspirations which he should have most near his heart. Despite this, and despite the truth of the comments made about him,

"Neither the son of his own country nor of any other."
"Scarcely human in fact."
"The victim of this faithless age" (p. 198),

he is "of some use as a journalist", and it is this usefulness that has forced him into the dilemma his position symbolises for him. He is a useful journalist, but only "turned journalist for the sake of Antonia's eyes" (p. 200). Consequently, the confusion of his moral perspectives is complete as far as his actions are concerned, despite his insistent efforts to keep them separate in his own mind.

> I am not deceiving myself about my motives. She won't leave Sulaco for my sake, therefore Sulaco must leave the rest of the Republic to its fate. Nothing could be clearer than that. I like a clearly defined situation. I cannot part with Antonia, therefore the one and indivisible Republic of Costaguana must be made to part with its western province. Fortunately it happens to be also a sound policy. The richest, the most fertile part of this land may be saved from anarchy. Personally, I care little, very little; but it's a fact that the establishment of Montero in power would mean death to me. In all the proclamations of general pardon which I have seen, my name, with a few others, is specially excepted (pp. 215–16).

Therefore, so that he will not have to be separated from his adored Antonia, he evolves a plan for the separation of Sulaco.

Now though the selfishness of Decoud's motives is quite intolerable from the point of view of public morality, one has to acknowledge and admire his own private morality for the sheer honesty involved in making such a statement, even to oneself. It is his love for Antonia which dictates to him the political expediency of war. But it is a war which will involve many others in needless hardship, and Decoud's real motives cannot possibly justify this. The immediate consequence of the adoption of his plan is that he can use the pretext of the silver's safety as an excuse for saving his own life without giving the appearance of running away, should Montero enter Sulaco. Indeed, Antonia's influence is such that it renders him incapable of running as far as Western Europe. Nevertheless, his presence on the lighter must be seen as an attempt to save his own skin. We might still believe in the altruism of Decoud's policy were it not for his letter home. He never seems to consider that his political measures may not make his wooing of Antonia successful. What neither he nor Nostromo can foresee are the private ends to which the silver will lead them both. Certainly they see it as something that might fight back at them, for Decoud says to Nostromo,

> "I can see it well enough myself, that the possession of this treasure is very much like a deadly disease for men situated as we are. But it had to be removed from Sulaco, and you were the man for the task" (p. 264).

But both are blind to the inevitability of their deaths once they have come into such close contact with the silver, for they consider only the nature of their cargo, and not their own. It is the moral outlooks of both which lead to their particular collapses.

Decoud, even at this stage, is acting only for private motives. Despite the approval of his political friends, the political advantage is not what is uppermost in his thoughts. Further we know that he has in his pocket a speech to be delivered at the Separation Ceremonies, and this makes us more than ever aware of the falsehood of his moral position. However much we may want to, Conrad never once lets us believe that Decoud is at all concerned with the safety of the Sulacans, or the prestige of the mine.

> The prospect of finding himself in the water and swimming, overwhelmed by ignorance and darkness, probably in a circle, till he sank from exhaustion, was revolting. The barren and cruel futility of such an end intimidated his affectation of careless pessimism (p. 282).

Such an end would not seem barren and cruel to someone who was acting first and foremost for the safety and welfare of others. To a person so motivated, it might even seem glorious. Its barrenness and futility are only apparent to one so motivated by his own personal desires that he cannot see the results of any action beyond those that affect him alone.

So we are led to the inevitable irony of Decoud's death, in all its actual barrenness and futility. As we now know, he has no real belief to see him through, and not even enough strength of will to go on living. In total self-realisation at last, he takes his own life.

The brilliant "Son Decoud," the spoiled darling of the family, the lover of Antonia and journalist of Sulaco, was not fit to grapple with himself single-handed. Solitude from mere outward condition of existence becomes very swiftly a state of soul in which the affectations of irony and scepticism have no place. It takes possession of the mind and drives forth the thought into the exile óf utter unbelief. After three days of waiting for the sight of some human face, Decoud caught himself entertaining a doubt of his own individuality (p. 497).

Decoud died from "solitude and want of faith in himself and others" (p. 496), "a victim of the disillusioned weariness which is the retribution meted out to intellectual audacity" (p. 501).

But Conrad is not concerned merely with the physical side of Decoud's death. As always, we are forced by a word or a phrase to acknowledge its significance in moral terms.

The vague consciousness of a misdirected life, given up to impulses whose memory left a bitter taste in his mouth was the first moral sentiment of his manhood (p. 498),

and we are compelled to accept the fact that Decoud's manipulation of politics for his own ends is the result of amorality, of having no worked-out scheme of conduct to guide him through the conflicting public and private issues of his life. But the author's comment does not rest with this. The hypocrisy of Decoud's life is reflected in the irony of the comments about him once he has died. He leaves, as it were, a legacy of empty statements, and the irony is increased because these statements would have endowed his memory with the most fulsome praise had his motives only been true to the appearance of his actions. Even Antonia is quite mistaken about him, for, talking of the possible annexation of the rest of Costaguana, she says

". . . this was from the first poor Martin's intention" (p. 509).

This is something we cannot accept. The pointlessness of allowing the political situation to go through a full circle to its original position is really only a side-issue here. Decoud was not interested in politics as the servant of the community, only as the servant of Decoud. Mitchell, also, is totally misled as to what he believes Decoud's plans to have been.

> Miss Avellanos burst into tears only when he told her how Decoud had happened to say that his plan would be a glorious success. ". . . And there's no doubt, sir, that it is. It is a success" (p. 489).

The mistake is to see the plan merely in terms of politics. Decoud saw them as the means, not the end. For others less selfishly motivated, politics were the end in themselves. For Decoud, the irony of his life has come home. To assess him adequately, we need only remember more of his own evaluation of himself.

> I am no more of a patriot than the Capataz of the Sulaco Cargadores, this Genoese who has done such great things for this harbour—this active usher-in of the material implements of progress (p. 191).

(iii)

Of the minor characters whom we must now discuss, Mitchell is clearly the most important in imparting an overall moral tone to the novel. Second to him is probably Hirsch. For Hirsch, small as his part is, has an important moral role to play. His first appearance provides yet another aspect of the overwhelming influence of material interests on Sulaco. But his significance within the novel quickly changes in the light of his cowardice and fear when he first meets Nostromo. This is further reinforced by his appearance on the silver-laden lighter, and by the manner of his subsequent removal onto Sotillo's steamer. Yet despite the innate cowardice of his nature and the pain of the *estrapade*, he summons up enough spiritual strength for a final act of defiance when he spits into Sotillo's face. This is not, however, where his actions end in importance. It is their conclusion which gives the whole episode added significance; for Sotillo, goaded into impetuosity, immediately shoots Hirsch. Thus he has deprived himself of his sole witness, and has put himself into a position where he has to fabricate a confession from Hirsch in order that he may justify his action in the eyes of his own officers. Hirsch, on the other hand, has found release not just from the pain of torture, but also from his own nature, from his cowardice and his constant worries on the subject of hides and of explosives. However acute his physical victimisation may have been, his one and only act of defiance provides him with a moral victory over Sotillo, who now must trust in Monygham's deceit to guide him to the silver.

If Hirsch can be described as the victim of his own imagination, Mitchell must surely be his exact opposite. Lacking imagination in the way that he does, it is not unjust to regard him as the Captain MacWhirr of *Nostromo*. Probably the greatest single example in the whole book of his lack of imagination is provided by his total failure to understand Monygham's motives in deceiving Sotillo. Mitchell's reaction is one of horror that Monygham could speak in such a way of a friend and a gentleman, for he is as pompous as he is unimaginative, and is always only too ready to stand on his dignity. His behaviour as a prisoner brings out, with magnificently achieved humour, his own feeling of self-importance. Against this, that is on the credit side of his personality as it were, we can place his trustworthiness; and his personal motto— "I'll have no mistakes here"—provides our first real insight into the depths of his character. Similarly, his captivity, as well as bringing us a breath of relief in its humorous application, also works to compel our admiration for him, despite both his pedantry and his pomposity. For we learn that

> For all his pomposity in social intercourse, Captain Mitchell could meet the realities of life in a resolute and ready spirit (p. 335).

He does this certainly, and in such a way as to terrify his captor Sotillo. Mitchell is here no longer a figure of fun, for within a matter of pages, Conrad's whole tone has changed in its treatment of him. He has stopped being the MacWhirr of the unrolled umbrella, and has become the MacWhirr of the typhoon.

> The old sailor, with all his small weaknesses and absurdities, was constitutionally incapable of entertaining for any length of time

a fear of his personal safety. It was not so much firmness of soul as the lack of a certain kind of imagination—the kind whose undue development caused intense suffering to Señor Hirsch (p. 338).

Because he is careless of himself in extremity, Mitchell reminds us most, by contrast, of Decoud. Decoud is now closeted with the silver alone on an island. Mitchell is occupying the strong room where the silver should have been. This both serves as an obvious link with Decoud, should we not have noticed the connection already, and also symbolises for us the worth of Mitchell in Conrad's estimation. He takes the place of the silver itself.

Unlike Decoud, or Hirsch, however, Mitchell does not really perform a direct and positive moral function in *Nostromo*. His technical usefulness in transferring the novel's climax away from the purely political issues of Sulaco's autonomy has already been remarked. Similarly, his narrative function is borne out further in the way that Mitchell provides us with information about Nostromo. Conrad achieves this in reverse, simply because we know how far Mitchell's interpretation of Nostromo's character is from the truth. Mitchell rightly prides himself on being the discoverer of Nostromo and for having appointed him to the position of Capataz de Cargadores. But he is blinded by his own pomposity and self-praise. Hence his final evaluation of Nostromo, the man, is important not because of what it tells us about Mitchell as a judge of human character, but because it allows us to see the difference between the appearance and the reality of Nostromo's motives.

> He carried all our lives in his pocket. Devotion, courage, fidelity, intelligence were not enough. Of course, he was perfectly fearless and incorruptible. But a man was wanted that would know how to succeed. He was that man, sir (pp. 482-3).

These are magnificent and laudatory epithets, but we know that they are not the whole story even of what Nostromo appears to be to those who surround him. Some, like Decoud, are deceived, it is true. Others are not so sure. But it is chiefly Mitchell who builds up for us the portrait of Nostromo which justifies his being nicknamed 'The Incorruptible'. Even at the end, after Nostromo has begun his process of becoming rich slowly, Mitchell is wholehearted in his praise of him.

"They could do no better than begin with the name of Nostromo. He has done for separation as much as anybody else, and," added Captain Mitchell, "has got less than many others by it—when it comes to that" (p. 482).

But from our omniscient positions as readers, we can immediately see the inaccuracy of such a comment, and can trace back from it the falsity of Mitchell's evaluation of his Capataz. In fact a close reading of the text shows us that Mitchell is not just wrong about Nostromo incidentally. Such a statement as "The fellow is devoted to me body and soul" might be merely a mistake in judgement. But it is really less innocuous than this. It is not simply that Mitchell never stops to examine Nostromo's motives. He makes positive use of Nostromo to bolster up his own pride and pomposity. To him, Nostromo

Clearly . . . was one of those invaluable subordinates whom to possess is a legitimate cause of boasting (p. 44).

Nevertheless, we must acknowledge that Nostromo is relatively central to the plot. He seems ever-present, appearing in all the incidents, as a general organiser and administrator for the railway, for rescuing Ribiera, and for arousing the Cargadores after one of their strikes; as the lover of the girls of Sulaco and as the protector of travellers and honest citizens. Mitchell again provides us with the information.

"This Nostromo, sir, a man absolutely above reproach, became the terror of all the thieves in the town" (p. 13).

But as with all Mitchell's analyses, this needs qualifying. It is obviously a vehicle for irony, for ultimately Nostromo is the greatest thief of any of them. This clearly shows the degree to which he is beyond reproach! We know too from Hirsch's account of his meeting with Nostromo, how well fitted the latter is for the role of brigand. The point, however, remains that he is not a thief, yet. And the manner of his theft has nothing of brigandage about it. It is as 'civilised' as one might expect it to be after the influence of the material interests from North America. The greatest tribute to Nostromo's all-round usefulness, however, is provided by the extent to which the leading citizens of Sulaco feel the need for him the moment he is believed drowned with the lighter.

(iv)

Even the intimacy of the night voyage on the lighter brings Decoud only halfway towards a proper understanding of his companion. He still believes him totally incorruptible, even in the presence of such wealth, and once again Conrad shows us clearly that such a judgement is as much a reflection on Decoud as on Nostromo himself.

> Decoud, incorrigible in his scepticism, reflected, not cynically, but with general satisfaction, that this man was made incorruptible by his enormous vanity, that finest form of egoism which can take on the aspect of every virtue (p. 300).

This is indeed an important forward step in our understanding of Nostromo's apparent virtues. Much earlier on Decoud had already commented on Nostromo's thirst for public recognition.

> His work is an exercise of personal powers; his leisure is spent in receiving the marks of extraordinary adulation. And he likes it, too. Can anybody be more fortunate? (p. 191).

His increased intimacy with Nostromo, however, does not give him any greater insight. His evaluation is purely external, and does not show the real nature of the man who "resented having been given a task in which there were so many chances of failure" (p. 275). None the less, his description of Nostromo is valuable in that it gives us a yardstick of the man's apparent personality, against which we can contrast the truth when we come to know it.

> He is more naïve than shrewd, more masterful than crafty, more generous with his personality than the people who make use of him are with their money. At least, that is what he thinks himself with more pride than sentiment. I am glad I have made friends

with him. As a companion he acquires more importance than he ever had as a sort of minor genius in his way—as an original Italian sailor whom I allowed to come in in the small hours and talk familiarly to the editor of the *Porvenir* while the paper was going through the press. And it is curious to have met a man for whom the value of life seems to consist in personal prestige (p. 248).

What Decoud in his own self-centredness fails to do is to question Nostromo's motives. He acknowledges the appearance of them, but goes no deeper. In this he does not even progress as far as Teresa Viola, wife of the staunch Garibaldino café-owner. She, it must be admitted, does not realise the full truth of her embittered taunts, hurled at the man on whom, invoked as a god, she has become so dependent, and on whom she has lavished all a mother's love for a desired son. Rightly she asserts that "he thinks of nobody but himself" (p. 20), and, with a mixture of truth and falsehood, tells him

"You have no heart, and you have no conscience, Gian' Battista——" (p. 23).

She provides us with a far more explicit picture of the situation which Decoud had half formulated while on board the lighter.

"He has not stopped very long with us. There is no praise from strangers to be got here," Signora Teresa said, tragically. "Avanti! Yes! That is all he cares for. To be first somewhere—somehow—to be first with these English. They will be showing him to everybody. 'This is our Nostromo!'" She laughed ominously (p. 23),

and it is because of the depth of her understanding that, despite her love for him, she makes, after he has refused to get her a priest, a prophecy about him the truth of which her death saves her from knowing.

"They have been paying you with words. Your folly shall betray you into poverty, misery, starvation" (p. 257).

The poverty, misery and starvation which Nostromo is ultimately going to suffer are neither literal nor physical. They are spiritual and moral. So it is his sense of having betrayed her, and the memory of her last words to him, that bring about in Nostromo the beginning of the emptiness of his existence, and the need for some reward for his exploits more positive than the noise of one's fellows which is called praise. That he turns for his reward to material substance is partly the influence of material interests on the land as a whole, and partly a result of his own mistaken judgement.

Monygham, too, is in part responsible for Nostromo's attempt at gaining a reward for himself by stealing the silver. We know from Nostromo's own confession to Decoud that he had originally come to Sulaco to "make his fortune" (p. 220). So far we have been led to believe that in Nostromo's eyes the praise of men amounts to fortune. But Monygham, unconsciously following Teresa Viola's indictment, influences Nostromo towards a change of opinion:

> ". . . for taking the curse of death upon my back, as you call it, nothing else but the whole treasure would do" (p. 259).

Now this change in attitude which has begun with Teresa's attempt at showing Nostromo the shallowness of his existence, is pushed on by Monygham, still the unwitting agent of Nostromo's change of heart, when he demonstrates to the Capataz the true solitariness of his position.

> "I went, indeed!" broke in Nostromo. "And for the sake of what—tell me?"
> "Ah! that is your own affair," the doctor said, roughly. "Do not ask me" (p. 430).

Despite then, or perhaps because of, the growth of his nagging realisation that spiritually he is an outcast, Nostromo shows not a little cunning in the way he hangs on to his secret knowledge of the whereabouts of the silver, and his bitterness eventually brings about a total reorientation of his motives. So, by the time that Nostromo has dissuaded the Doctor from advising Sotillo to search the Great Isabel for the silver, he too has changed from being the devoted servant of public affairs, and is now loyal only to his private self. Along with this narrowing of moral perspectives, that is since he no longer sees any value in serving public ends and finding his own personal reward simply in so doing, Nostromo, perhaps because he is betraying the greater moral outlook, himself becomes obsessed with the notions of betrayal and loneliness. To Monygham he says,

> "I do not suppose that you would hasten to give me up to Sotillo, for example. It is not that. It is that I am nothing! Suddenly——" He swung his arm downwards. "Nothing to anyone," he repeated (p. 454).

His world has become a vacuity, for, most of all, he has become nothing to himself.

This notion of betrayal which is one of the biggest of the factors contributing to the theft of the silver, stays with Nostromo right up to the time of his death. Speaking of Giselle, he says, thinking most of his own lack of faith,

> "She would not have betrayed me. . . . She was faithful. We were going very far—very soon. I could have torn myself away from that accursed treasure for her. For that child I would have left boxes and boxes of it—full. And Decoud took four. Four ingots. Why? *Picardia!* To betray me? How could I give back the treasure with four ingots missing? They would have said I had purloined them. The doctor would have said that. Alas! it holds me yet!" (p. 559).

It is not, as he seems to think, betrayal by others that has caused Nostromo's downfall. It is he who has betrayed others. So he becomes obsessed with the fact that he has betrayed "the soul of a woman and the life of a man" (*v.* p. 502). 'The Incorruptible' has in fact been corrupted by the natural extensions of those values whose development we have just now been tracing. Nothing can dispel his sense of grievance against the world at large, not even the glory of the famous ride to Cayta. So the events of his life bring him to an acute self-realisation. Waking up after his swim,

> He felt the pinch of poverty for the first time in his life. To find himself without money after a run of bad luck at *monte* in the low, smoky room of Domingo's posada, where the fraternity of Cargadores gambled, sang, and danced of an evening; to remain with empty pockets after a burst of public generosity to some

peyne d'oro girl or other (for whom he did not care), had none of
the humiliation of destitution. He remained rich in glory and
reputation. But since it was no longer possible for him to parade
the streets of the town, and be hailed with respect in the usual
haunts of his leisure, this sailor felt himself destitute indeed
(p. 415).

Spurred on by this feeling of destitution, Nostromo blames
the rich and also the material interests which he believes to
have forced his exile onto him. This attitude shows the first
real signs that he considers his own self. Conrad shows us his
incapacity, when alone, nourishing his sense of betrayal. So
unavoidably Nostromo makes for the town and for his meeting with Monygham.

It is not, however, just a sense of betrayal which takes
possession of Nostromo.

The magnificent Capataz de Cargadores, deprived of certain
simple realities, such as the admiration of women, the adulation
of men, the admired publicity of his life, was ready to feel the
burden of sacrilegious guilt descend upon his shoulders (p. 420).

He can no longer find compensation and happiness in the
old way. Teresa had ruined all that for him. Although his
"name is known from one end of Sulaco to the other" (p. 489),
even this does not save him from becoming the "victim of
the disenchanted vanity which is the reward of audacious
action" (p. 501). Because he has betrayed "first a woman, then
a man, abandoned each in their last extremities for the sake
of this accursed treasure" (p. 502), he needs some new justification. So it is the treasure itself which finally comes to
possess him, and claim him as its victim.

"There is something in a treasure that fastens upon a man's mind.
He will pray and blaspheme and still persevere, and will curse
the day he ever heard of it, and will let his last hour come upon
him unawares, still believing that he missed it only by a foot. He
will see it every time he closes his eyes. He will never forget it till
he is dead— . . . There is no getting away from a treasure that
once fastens upon your mind" (p. 460).

There is one final aspect of Nostromo's personality which
must be dealt with before we come to make our final statements about him. His isolation becomes complete in propor-

131

tion to the degree of confusion his moral values suffer. He is humiliated in having to act by stealth alone. It is not just the silver that tortures him, either. His loneliness, like Razumov's, becomes the less bearable because he can have no confidant. We, the readers, are the only ones who know the whole truth of his secret. Even his last ally, Mrs Gould, knows only a small fraction of the whole, while Giselle, his love, can have no inkling of his reason for returning to the island. Giselle here acts also as a counterbalance, for she is so much more faithful than her lover, in that she cares for him as a person, and not for what he does or how he does it. In this way she allies herself with Mrs Gould and Monygham in their concern for personal relationships.

It should be remembered that Nostromo is the only character in the whole novel who knows about the silver, or who can begin to understand what happened to Decoud. The fact that these things are not hidden from him, as they are from everyone else, reflects directly, and symbolises the conflict between appearance and reality which dominates his moral being. Although he may not be completely central to the plot of the novel, he is absolutely central to its moral structure. So his death, which comes as the indirect outcome of his moral values, provides the climax for the novel as a whole. His moral confusion is embedded in the fact that he has become unable to reconcile his public and private values. As we first see him, he is privately happy, that is, he is happy as a person, with what he publicly appears to be to others. But Teresa Viola was the agent who engendered in him a dissatisfaction with his world of appearances. None the less, there had been nothing wrong with this morality, for it had not been founded on deception. His public self was based on a sound private morality. After his so-called enlightenment by Teresa, however, Nostromo made a wrong moral decision, and one which was ultimately to prove fatal to him. Instead of retaining his own scheme of values and altering the appearance of his life so that it still fitted in with it, he retained the outward show but with an altered and inadequate ethical backing. In other words, he continued his appearance of serving public ends while in reality he was acting for private gain, with a scheme of almost total self-seeking. Previously he had found satisfaction, private satisfaction that is, in the service of public issues. So, as long as private served public, he was famous, successful, and content. Significantly, this fame did not leave him when his values changed, but his own sense of satisfaction did; and his collapse, in this case physical as well as moral, became inevitable.

Within this topic of the interplay between appearance and reality, Nostromo is the exact opposite of Monygham. In what virtually constitutes an immoral manner, Nostromo uses the appearance of serving others as a camouflage for the theft, and thus for immoral ends. Monygham on the other hand appears churlish and totally wrapped up in himself. In fact, he uses any means possible to further the good of others, whatever the cost to himself.

(v)

We have now looked at some of the moral protagonists of the novel. If their significance is to be fully appreciated, however, their values must be viewed within the much larger framework of the novel as a whole.

Material interests are almost personified by their missionary in Sulaco, Holroyd. In treating the San Tomé mine as a hobby, which is what he does, he becomes for us the embodiment of outside commercial interests. This has the further effect of reminding us of a refined yet no less insidious type of that sort of exploitation which Conrad had written of in *Heart of Darkness*. Holroyd's whole outlook, even down to its religious side, is a product of the harsh and impersonal world of commerce. Personal values mean nothing to him. As Mrs Gould pointed out, he even regards God as a sort of business partner, and significantly enough the evangelical buildings of the San Tomé settlement are 'recognisably American' (p. 103) in their architecture. His missionary work is carried out in order to keep his partnership with his evangelical God on good terms.

"Mr Holroyd's sense of religion," Mrs Gould pursued, "was shocked and disgusted at the tawdriness of the dressed-up saints in the cathedral—the worship, he called it, of wood and tinsel. But it seemed to me that he looked upon his own God as a sort of influential partner, who gets his share of profits in the endowment of churches" (p. 71).

This underlines the fact that Holroyd is interested in things, not people, in the future, not the past, however glorious that past may be in its traditions.

"We can't give you your ecclesiastical court back again; but you shall have more steamers, a railway, a telegraph-cable—a future in the great world which is worth infinitely more than any amount of ecclesiastical past" (p. 36).

This is for us the final statement of where his values lie. Progress can only be material in his eyes. It does not consist in using material improvements and technological advances for the betterment of the people's condition, and we shall see that his influence here is widespread. As one would expect, it is seen chiefly in the way that it affects Charles Gould. He, it should be remembered, had inherited the Gould Concession from a father who, in his son's eyes, had been tackling the whole thing wrongly. But before the silver became merely a pawn in the political games, Charles had not been blind to the possibilities of the silver serving the needs of an oppressed people.

The cruel futility of things stood unveiled in the levity and sufferings of that incorrigible people; the cruel futility of lives and of deaths thrown away in the vain endeavour to attain an enduring solution of the problem (p. 364).

When we first meet him, Gould is an idealist, and his idealism is not just for turning the mine into a working concern. He sees the silver as the future servant of Sulacans and Costaguaneros. In this way he lends hope to the idealism of Don José Avellanos, and supports and fosters that of his wife. But at once he is on dangerous ground, for, in taking over the mine, he is taking over what had previously been a symbol of tyranny and oppression. The statement about its previous closure read,

"Justly incensed at the grinding oppression of foreigners, actuated by sordid motives of gain rather than by love for a country where they come impoverished to seek their fortunes, the mining population of San Tomé, etc. . . ." (p. 52).

Although the wording of this looks forward to Gould's own later obsession with the mine, at present it shows only the idealism of his motives. With the emergence of the mine as a dramatic force in his life, he has evolved a moral scheme for the mine's use, and moral ideas for the results of the mine's efficient and economical working.

> What is wanted here is law, good faith, order, security. Any one can declaim about these things, but I pin my faith to material interests. Only let the material interests once get a firm footing, and they are bound to impose the conditions on which alone they can continue to exist. That's how your money-making is justified here in the face of lawlessness and disorder. It is justified because the security which it demands must be shared with an oppressed people. A better justice will come afterwards (p. 84).

This is Gould's sole justification morally, but it is important to recognise that he sees the need for a moral justification. He recognises the dangerous qualities of material interests, but, unlike Holroyd, sees that this danger will have to be gripped if the population is ultimately to benefit. It is in the hope of using the mine to improve the conditions of the native population that Gould supports the political regime of the enlightened Ribiera. This dabbling in politics represents Gould's public morality, and we must also realise that this public front is supported quite genuinely by what Gould's personal feelings are. In other words, the public morality involved is wholly supported by the private. There is not any discrepancy between the two. Later in the novel, even, when Gould has undergone a moral change and only the appearances of former times are kept, Antonia can say to him,

> "It is your character that is the inexhaustible treasure which may save us all yet; your character, Carlos, not your wealth. I entreat you to give this man your word that you will accept any arrangement my uncle may make with their chief. One word. He will want no more" (p. 361).

Such is Gould's personal prestige even after the collapse of Ribiera. Even after an obsession with the mine simply for its

own sake has begun to take posession of him, he retains traces
of his former idealism. Although he saw that there was no
turning back, he retained something of his humanitarian
vision.

> "It was Don Pépé who called the gorge the Paradise of snakes.
> No doubt we have disturbed a great many. But remember, my
> dear, that . . . It is no longer a Paradise of snakes. We have
> brought mankind into it, and we cannot turn our backs upon
> them to go and begin a new life elsewhere" (p. 209).

He is fully aware still of his obligation to his human
dependants.

But not for long. Charles Gould's moral perspectives
become severely limited under the influence of the mine, as
his father's life had done physically. This, as I have already
tried to suggest, is the direct result of obsession, that is of
allowing the issue of the mine itself to exclude from one's
outlook all other issues. The clearest words on the development of this obsession in Gould are probably Monygham's.

> "There is no peace and no rest in the development of material
> interests. They have their law and their justice. But it is founded
> on expediency, and is inhuman; it is without rectitude, without
> the continuity and the force that can be found only in a moral
> principle . . . the time approaches when all that the Gould
> Concession stands for shall weigh as heavily upon the people as
> the barbarism, cruelty, and misrule of a few years back" (p. 511).

So Gould's obsession means that his moral principles, which
embraced the welfare of all those concerned with the mine
and many more, have yielded to expediency. His title, the
'King of Sulaco', becomes ominous only because he is no
longer motivated solely for the good of the people, and
Decoud's statement about him thus takes on a horrible truth.

> "He cannot act or exist without idealizing every simple feeling,
> desire, or achievement. He could not believe his own motives if
> he did not make them first a part of some fairy tale. The earth is
> not quite good enough for him, I fear" (pp. 214–15).

The truth of this is irrefutable. For the sake of the mine,
Gould rejects the world, including his own wife. His attitude

of 'mine or nothing', which so terrifies Hirsch when he is making enquiries about dynamite, should have no less an effect on us. Gould has done nothing more than idealise "the existence, the worth, the meaning of the San Tomé mine" (p. 214), and we learn further that he has now only one motive,

> the safety of the San Tomé mine with the preservation of the Gould Concession in the spirit of his compact with Holroyd (p. 317)

—in the spirit, that is, of material interests. They have become an end in themselves.

So, along with everything else, Charles Gould rejects Sulaco, its needs, its inhabitants and its politics. None the less, his old ideals still influence what he says, though his criticisms are now wholly destructive. He has lost the will to improve and mend. When Don Juste Lopez asks him to join the deputation which will welcome Pedrito Montero into the city, he answers

> "My advice, señores, is that you should wait for your fate in your houses. There is no necessity for you to give yourselves up for-mally into Montero's hands. Submission to the inevitable, as Don Juste calls it, is all very well, but when the inevitable is called Pedrito Montero there is no need to exhibit pointedly the whole extent of your surrender. The fault of this country is the want of measure in political life. Flat acquiescence in illegality, followed by sanguinary reaction—that, señores, is not the way to a stable and prosperous future" (p. 367).

These words are ironic, certainly, but more than this they connote an immorality which is made the more pointed for us because Don Juste has brought the little frightened deputation to Gould simply because he is controller of what happens at the mine, and because the mine was

> the most stable, the most effective force they had ever known to exist in their province (p. 368).

In parenthesis it is worth contrasting Gould's attitude at the time immediately preceding Montero's entry into Sulaco with the attitudes of the mine's two custodians. Don Pépé's sense of humour and Father Roman's simplicity react superbly against each other, but they also work together to form a composite whole. For it is from these two that we gain our yardstick against which we can judge Gould's behaviour. To Gould the mine means silver. As an assessment this is of course naïve, but it provides a convenient label for his obsession just with the mine. He is not predominantly bothered about the silver as silver, that is for the wealth it means to him, or to others. It is just the continued working of the mine itself which matters. However, Don Pépé and the Padré see the mine rather in terms of the people who work there, and who live in its three villages. Significantly, it is their values, not Gould's, which save the situation when the miners themselves march upon the town at the very hour when Gould himself is led out by the occupying forces, who intend to shoot him.

Despite the fact that it is not he who had saved the mine, but the people of the mine who had saved him, Gould remains inflexible in his attitude. After Montero's defeat, Charles ignores this lesson, and so completely fails to reorientate his values. We know that the existence of the mine depends entirely on Gould's safety, and this fact looks outward to a situation of much wider perspectives where the mine's existence means the founding of a new state, and, however good and laudatory an event this may be in the abstract, we cannot but reject those values which led up to its occurrence. Gould's position is very similar to Nostromo's in that he never lets slip the façade of his altruistic moral idealism. The true inner reality we glean mostly from Monygham and Mrs Gould, both of whom see exactly what is happening to Charles, and how much his belief in being the chief benefactor of the community in terms of people has become mere façade.

(vi)

Many references have been made already to Mrs Gould, and to the way in which she both is an agent of moral insight, and helps us to retain our moral perspectives when reading

Nostromo. This, however, does not do her full justice as one of the greatest of Conrad's artistic creations. So it is to a discussion of her that we must now finally turn. As already suggested, 'Dona Emilia' is the character who first makes us examine the morality of that sort of progress brought about solely by the undiscriminating use of materialism. From the outset, it is she who realises the sort of personal destruction which progress—in this particular instance the railway—means. Her attitude is here symbolised by the way in which she is instrumental in preserving the Casa Viola from imminent but needless demolition. Similarly, her painting of the Paradise of Snakes in its original state when man has been already catered for there, symbolises her sorrow at the destruction of the natural environment for the sake of this material progress.

This particular aspect of the whole concept of progress, that is its material application only, faces us yet again later in the novel when there is talk of the annexation of the rest of Costaguana. Answering Antonia's comment which arises from her mistaken beliefs about Decoud that "this was from the first poor Martin's intention" (p. 509), Dr Monygham crystallises the whole position for us.

> "The material interests will not let you jeopardise their development for a mere idea of pity and justice," the doctor muttered, grumpily (p. 509).

This is indeed the pass to which things have come. Material interests have taken over. The conspiracy must inevitably never be born because it is of concern only to those few who care about suffering human beings, and not to those people whom Conrad ironically shows to command the greater importance, the controllers of material interests. A new state can emerge if it is a question of saving the mine. But material interests are no longer considered as possessing the primary function of serving and relieving the poor and the oppressed. From this, two things become apparent. One is the difference between Mr and Mrs Gould which has been touched on in passing but which will be considered in more detail next. The other is the close alliance in the artistic concern of the novel between moral theme and the concept of progress. Both of these are anchored to the overall framework of material interests in which the novel itself exists. As already suggested, Gould is the central figure of this particular framework—the king-pin of it all. We have already remarked how he began, idealistically enough, working, as he hoped, for the good of the people; and this tradition is maintained and upheld by his wife even after he has let it drop. For his original aim, that of progress in human terms, becomes lost because he is overwhelmed by the negativism of his own morality. The impersonality of his moral orientation, and the way he himself seems to become something less than human, is thrown into sharper profile simply because of his wife's concern for human relationships. The growth of this rift between the Goulds is of course the reason for Mrs Gould's never disclosing Nostromo's secret of the whereabouts of the silver. Gould has probably never even noticed that a rift has grown between them, and Emily—we can call her by her English name now —will have noticed that too, much to her increased disappointment. So she rejects the impersonalising influence of the silver, knowing how it has corrupted Nostromo and suspecting what it has done to Decoud. Instead, she can cherish the return of human warmth which she herself brought to Nostromo's deathbed, and which allowed him to shed onto her the one thing that was still tormenting him.

It would be wrong therefore to suggest that Emily Gould serves merely to pinpoint the different definitions of progress contained in the book. Her function is much more positive than this, for, as is shown by the scene at Nostromo's death, she is most of all concerned with humanity, and with those values that are spiritual rather than material. Whereas Mitchell provides us with a sort of basic unimaginative morality, Emily is the positive spiritual power behind the whole novel. Even while her husband is falling prey to his obsession, she sees Sulaco as it is

> . . . a great land of plain and mountain and people, suffering and mute, waiting for the future in a pathetic immobility of patience (p. 88).

From the start we know that "she was guided by an alert perception of values" (p. 46), and, from our earlier discussions here, that her interpretation of progress is in solely human terms. To her, therefore, people are what is of paramount importance. This is shown by her every relationship, with each person who shares the environment with her. Similarly, she is not deceived as to what people really are by their outward appearances. Monygham's forbidding external personality is immaterial to her. She knows that the inner man is good. Again when she hears of the death of Decoud, her first thought is not for him, but for Antonia. Perhaps she suspected his motives in accompanying the silver. At any rate the incident allows Conrad to stress, through her, the importance of the present over the past, and the living over the dead. This does not mean that Emily rejects tradition and the past wholeheartedly as does Holroyd. Indeed, one needs to remember that she rates him for just this. The difference between them is in the application of their views to human beings. What use are Holroyd's evangelical missions when the native inhabitants find faith and comfort in their primitive statues? Emily sees this, and shows here again the past as servant of the present, but in solely human terms.

It is important to recognise that Emily's actions are completely altruistic despite any incidental rewards she may gain. She was instrumental in obtaining silver spectacles for Giorgio Viola because of those same motives that we have already seen when she arranged for the preservation of his home. It is the result of simple affection for the old man, not that of some sort of calculating foreknowledge that his gratitude would one day urge him to exhort Nostromo to the assistance of the Goulds' silver. Indeed her concern for others has such power as to be infectious to those who are not too insensitive to feel it. Even the engineer made the famous railway ride to Cayta possible only "for the sake of the Goulds" (p. 482). When Emily concerns herself at all over the mine, it is to think of that too in terms of human beings, as did Don Pépé. Hence her interpretation of its social role, already much stressed here, as well as in *Nostromo* itself, that the mine must be an instrument of welfare.

But it is perhaps in her attitude to Hernandez that we can see most clearly her perception in terms of the human situation. In fact she sees right through the veil of political intrigue and propaganda to the truth at the heart of the matter.

"If it had not been for the lawless tyranny of your Government, Done Pépé, many an outlaw now with Hernandez would be living peaceably and happy at the honest work of his hands" (p. 109),

and, as if to provide further evidence of the truth of her insight, many Sulacans—Don José Avellanos among them— flock to Hernandez to escape the ferocity of a Montero. We know too that the so-called fearsome brigand "could not have been coming back on an errand of injustice and oppression" (p. 358). As if to cast into yet further relief the enlightenment Mrs Gould has shown in this respect, all the lights in the town are extinguished as she disappears into her house after having said goodbye to Don José. Once Hernandez becomes a general, his fitness for such a post becomes fully apparent, despite the irony of Mitchell's vision of him. For his morality is an absolute one, founded on value based on worth, and free from political intrigue. This is why Conrad can tell us that Antonia

would entrust the last day—the last hours perhaps—of her father's life to the keeping of the bandit, whose existence was a protest against the irresponsible tyranny of all parties alike, against the moral darkness of the land (pp. 353–4).

Yet only by suppressing the evidence of the novel itself could we avoid acknowledging that Emily Gould becomes herself a victim in a way quite as acute as either Nostromo or Decoud. Indeed this stems from the spirituality of her moral enlightenment which we have been just now discussing. What makes her in many ways the most wretched of the three is that her unhappiness derives from an external source. It does not stem from within her own person as do Nostromo's and Decoud's. If it derives from any single individual at all, it is Charles Gould who must be held to account for it. One remembers how, in the initial situation, the silver is a symbol for goodness to husband and wife alike.

> For them both, each passing of the escort under the balconies of the Casa Gould was like another victory gained in the conquest of peace for Sulaco (p. 115).

This is their joint aim. Consequently the change in national values which accompanies the coming of the Ribiera regime is a source of great happiness to her. She sees the mine's financial backing of the regime as their joint personal contribution to national welfare.

> "All this brings nearer the sort of future we desire for the country, which has waited for it in sorrow long enough, God knows" (p. 120).

Nevertheless, her joy is short-lived. Nor did it blind her to the importance of personal qualities. She knows that, however noble and right-minded the aims, the promoter must have enough conviction, enough strength of character to see them through. So,

> she was made uneasy. He was more pathetic than promising, this first civilian Chief of the State Costaguana had ever known, pronouncing, glass in hand, his simple watchwords of honesty, peace, respect for law, political good faith abroad and at home— the safeguards of national honour (p. 119).

Because we have learnt this, we are not surprised at the collapse of the regime in the face of rather more ruthless opposition. Mrs Gould's reaction at the failure of what the mine had supported is totally different from her husband's. This is where the rift which we have already commented on between them begins to develop. For while Gould, presumably seeking consolation for this setback, turns to the mine itself, she admits the failure, acknowledges its cause, but refuses to modify her ideals one jot.

> Mrs Gould had no silver mine to look after. In the general life of the Gould Concession she was represented by her two lieutenants, the doctor and the priest, but she fed her woman's love for excitement on events whose significance was purified to her by the fire of her imaginative purpose (p. 149).

In other words, of the two of them, her faith is much the stronger, for she remains loyal to her cause, longing to keep the mine independent of the intrigues of power politics, and thus morally unsullied. He resigns his interest in the good of the world outside the mine in the face of one setback. Unlike his, her perspective moves far enough back from the issues surrounding the mine to see that it is neither benefiting Gould himself, nor doing the natives the hoped-for good. Monygham thus becomes soul-mate of her disappointment, for he has the knowledge of human nature to lament Gould's lack of insight into his own domestic situation.

> He could follow her silent thought. Was it for this that her life had been robbed of all the intimate felicities of daily affection which her tenderness needed as the human body needs air to breathe? And the doctor, indignant with Charles Gould's blindness, hastened to change the conversation (p. 512).

There is this bond of sympathy between them simply because they share the same forces of motivation, and because they have the same sort of background of past experiences. We have discussed already the doctor's sufferings and moral degradation which form the basis of his character. To realise that the physical defects left by this torture are of little significance to him, we need only recall the readiness with which he was prepared to face Sotillo's fury, even against the knowledge of what happened to Hirsch. Mrs Gould, too, acts from a background of spiritual suffering, and possibly even mental cruelty.

> "... this house I love. It has seen all my life."
> "Ah, yes!" snarled the doctor, suddenly. "Women count time from the marriage feast. Didn't you live a little before?"
> "Yes; but what is there to remember? There were no cares."
> Mrs Gould sighed (p. 507).

For this reason alone, the selflessness of her nature makes her want to relieve the sufferings of others. This is the fundamental of her credo and at the same time the reason for the cry of her nightmares, "Material Interests." Even at the end, when she comes so closely into contact with Nostromo, that other great victim of material interests in the novel, she refuses to divulge his secret, and talks to him chiefly about his contacts with people, about his behaviour towards Linda and Giselle.

Unlike Nostromo, however, and despite her sufferings and her victimisation, Mrs Gould survives. This again is in support of our interpretation of her as the agent representing the positive side of morality, and counteracting the negativism of the other moral schemes shown in the novel. Her unity of purpose is the really vital thing about her. The whole novel acts or reacts in perspective to this.

But what ensures her survival in this environment which seems so hostile to her? Two things: THE fact that she stands for the spiritual value of a thing rather than the material, and, a development of this, her concern for personal relationships. It is because of the first of these that she knows the harmfulness of the silver, and especially the stolen silver, and so keeps the secret to herself. But without the central issue of the material interests around which the whole plot revolves, her spiritual values might never have grown into the insight which she shows into the workings of the world of commerce.

> It had come into her mind that for life to be large and full, it must contain the care of the past and of the future in every passing moment of the present. Our daily work must be done to the glory of the dead, and for the good of those who come after (pp. 520–1).

This doctrine comes as the result of her experiences in Costaguana, despite the universality of its application. It is the final stage in the development of her ideals, which one can trace right the way through. One recalls at once the halfway stage to this in her words to Monygham.

> "Things seem to be worth nothing by what they are in themselves. I begin to believe that the only solid thing about them is the spiritual value which everyone discovers in his own form of activity——" (p. 318).

A couple of paragraphs ago I remarked that there was, however, a second factor in Mrs Gould's survival, her relationships

CONRAD AND THE HUMAN DILEMMA

with others. The relative success or failure of all the characters in the novel is closely correlated to the spiritual value
which each discovers or, in some cases fails to discover, in
his own form of activity. And this answers the problem of the
mine itself. In what sense can it be called a success? Clearly
within the framework of the novel, such an impersonality
as a mine can be neither a success nor a failure in terms
of moral values. It is what the mine stands for that we shall
have to discuss shortly. If for the moment, however, we return
to those moral groupings I suggested at the outset of this
discussion, we will see that Conrad rejects all but one, the
one which views the mine physically only in terms of human
beings involved, and spiritually in terms of its potential for
human welfare. So, leaving alone those groups which either
fail or are rejected by Conrad, we are left with that which
comprises the Avellanos, Mrs Gould, Dr Monygham, and,
surprisingly, Giselle. Her we must include because of her
concern, unlike that of her sister, for Nostromo the man himself, not the hero or the villain in the light of his actions.
These then are the only characters who can be said to survive
in any way more than the purely physical one, and can thus
be seen to have Conrad's approval and therefore to represent
his positives.

(vii)

Having spent all this time analysing character and motivation
in *Nostromo*, we are now at the stage of being able to ask
where does all this get us. Because of the domination of the
mine symbolising the material interests which cause suffering,
moral decay and unhappiness, we can only regard Sulaco as
a moral failure, simply because capitalism has made it as
unpleasant as anywhere else for the people who live there.
Only characters like Mitchell, who avowedly is totally without imagination, have not the awareness to see what has
happened. Every character in the novel is influenced for the
worse, and everywhere, happiness, that most personal of all
qualities, has been forced into submission to materialism. Nostromo and Decoud are utterly destroyed; Antonia

146

Avellanos is forced into permanent mourning. The Violas suffer as much as anyone else, for even the Isabels are tarnished. For Nostromo himself the lure has been absolutely fatal. Long before it killed him in a bodily sense, it sapped away at his spiritual being with the insidiousness of all parasites. But Conrad does not let Captain Fidanza, as Nostromo calls himself towards the end of the novel, lose total prestige in our eyes. For he realises what has happened to him. He is powerless to resist. There is no question of that. But he understands. This is the first great step he makes towards his moral redemption. He confesses to Emily Gould. This is not entirely like Razumov. Psychologically, it is true, the burden of his guilt is too much for him, and he needs to share it. But this is not the most important thing about his confession. What it symbolises, and what it is so utterly vital to us to realise, is that he has seen what has happened to himself. In being seduced by the silver, he has yielded himself up, admittedly not without a struggle, to material interests.

The second thing he realises, and this is what completes his redemption in spiritual terms, is shown by his statement that he would have left the silver for the sake of Giselle. In general terms this is a symbolic utterance also. Nostromo has seen that personal relationships are the most important things in life beyond the possession of a stable morality. His realisation of this can be traced back to his guilt feelings, at first unanalysed however acutely felt, at the betrayal of Viola's wife and of Decoud. This at first eats into his heart and causes bitterness because, in a way that is entirely human, he will not at first acknowledge that he had behaved badly. With his statement of love for Giselle, all this is redeemed, and though we feel loss and pity at his death, we can feel some measure of comfort and consolation in his having not died before he achieved spiritual wholeness.

That leaves us with only the positive group to discuss. What is the relationship between the silver and those characters whom Conrad so approves as to make them the combatants of materialism? We have seen Monygham and Mrs Gould working against the materialism of the mine in spiritual terms, but in terms of physical reality they are virtually powerless. So Mrs Gould is left comfortable in a worldly sense, but desperately unhappy. This is of course the power of the mine again. She is spiritually estranged from her husband, for on this level her only companion is, as we have seen, Monygham. The spirit of materialism which has pervaded the whole book has power even over those of exemplary goodness. This is where its power really lies and, in its insight, it is where much of the power of the book lies. There is no happy ending by which we can find relief from the world of harsh reality. For materialism is the reality of our age. This is Conrad's warning. None can escape. Partial exemption only can be found by the guiding principles arising from spiritual values. Only from these can we derive any hope at all.

5

Conclusion

THERE is, I think, a very real danger in attempting to write a concluding chapter to a discussion of this sort. Since each novel which has been examined is a separate work of art, having its own separate entity and its own values, the exercise of discovering categories and making generalisations which can be applied to all three is more likely to be of harm than value. For even within a single author, books are unlikely to stand for the same values, unless the author is repeating himself to a very large extent throughout his writings. Similarly, as far as these three Conrad novels are concerned, an attempt to find common factors may well turn out to be an irrelevant pursuit. None the less, there is a degree of consistency in Conrad's moral outlook which would suggest that in his case the views of the man coincide with the views of the artist, and it is this which not only justifies some drawing together of ideas at the end of this volume, but rather necessitates it. In this particular instance, there are ideas which are central to all three novels, and are therefore of the utmost relevance to our study. We have seen, of course—how could we fail to see it?—the development of an overall moral perspective out of character, and from the interplay between characters themselves and between character and environment. We have also seen the difficulties, alluded to in the introduction, that tend to arise when a character inclines towards amorality. He has no foundations which can help him in the true guiding of his actions, so when he is faced with a problem or a difficulty which is anything other than purely physical, he has no idea what rightness involves.

(i)

When regarded overall the Political Novels, as already suggested, deal with a far more complex existence than the Sea

Novels. In the latter, conflict is often merely the conflict of the two moralities; public and private. But the environment of them is still that in which survival, spiritual survival that is, is a very real possibility. The world of the sea is much more attractive to Conrad than that of the land largely because it is morally much more secure.

> And suddenly I rejoiced in the great security of the sea as compared with the unrest of the land, in my choice of that untempted life presenting no disquieting problems, invested with an elementary moral beauty by the absolute straight-forwardness of its appeal and by the singleness of its purpose ('The Secret Sharer', in *'Twixt Land and Sea Tales,* p. 96).

This quotation shows with great clarity the nature of Conrad's ideal moral situation. What appeals to him is not of course the beauty he refers to here. That is merely an aesthetic extension of the fact that the situation he describes in these words is an absolute one, providing a moral code for behaviour which will ensure survival. However, the Political Novels at first seem to suggest nothing so positive, for they portray a different sort of human dilemma. The conflict here is not one of man combating the elements, or even alternatively of man against man. More particularly the supreme conflict which lies at the centre of the drama of these three novels is that of man combating himself. And this is what provides the total antithesis to the 'absolute straightforward-ness' and 'singleness of purpose' mentioned in the quotation from 'The Secret Sharer'. It is that same aspect of life on shore to which Matthew Arnold refers in *The Scholar Gypsy.*

> . . . this strange disease of modern life,
> With its sick hurry, its divided aims,
> Its heads o'ertaxed, its palsied hearts . . .

This diversity of motivation is the crucial thing to our understanding of what Conrad's moralising is about. This discussion of the novels has stressed the concepts of motivation, morality and expediency. We must not, in doing this, allow this commentary to leave us with the notion that Conrad's portrayal of the human dilemma is entirely pessimistic.

CONCLUSION

(ii)

The Secret Agent's pessimism is the pessimism of characters within the novel. Conrad's bearing on the work of art as a whole will not stand up to being interpreted as pessimism. To make this distinction clear Conrad has shown us in Winnie the power of an amoral nobility which, because of its very amorality, culminates in self-destruction. But the amorality in Winnie is merely a reflection of the amorality of the whole society of *The Secret Agent*. To amplify this here would be merely to repeat what has already been written in Chapter 2. All we need to add now is that the pessimism which must emerge from the lives of the characters in this particular novel is a quality arising directly from their motivation.

This relates closely to the ironic mode which is so predominant in these novels. We shall again be guilty of misinterpretation if we interpret Conrad's use of irony as an indication that morality is of necessity an ironic subject to him. This is not the point. Only deviations from morality, those codes of behaviour which in these pages have been defined as immorality and amorality, are ironic. For it is the supreme irony that, in acting against morality out of what is ultimately nothing more than self-interest, the characters are, in the final analysis, being their own worst enemies. Winnie is again the supreme instance of this. She is the centre of Stevie's world, and it is her complex motivation which forces Stevie onto Verloc and destroys all three of them. Compared to Stevie's, the deaths of the Verlocs are unimportant. For Stevie is the moral innocent, the simple and sincere victim.

This simplicity at the artistic centre of *The Secret Agent* is reflected in the simplicity at the narrative centre of *Under Western Eyes*. Again, one is aware of the dangers of repeating oneself, but the risk must be taken if the novels are successfully to be related to each other. One cannot but remark again on the isolation of the narrator-Professor. Westerner as he is, he is removed from the confusions of the Easterners he observes. But this is not merely a physical phenomenon. It is a moral one as well. Throughout, his moral creed is sincere, simple and whole. It is this that never allows us to forget, even for an instant, the necessity for a true and simple moral orientation, worked out, ready for life, which Razumov lacks every bit as much as Verloc did.

The essential message at the heart of both these novels is simply that no form of self-indulgence is an answer for anything beyond the immediate expedience of the present. Only the denial of the self in a pure and simple way can bring moral wholeness and happiness. This is the difference in success between Emily Gould and Winnie Verloc. But we must not let our concern for character throughout these pages blind us to the fact that simplicity and sincerity are equally as important to moral wholeness as self-denial. If this were not so, our reading would make nonsense of *The Secret Agent*'s insight into Winnie. This is what is of direct relevance to us for it provides us not only with an emotional reaction aroused by Winnie's death at the end of the novel, but also with a moral scheme for the real world as well as for the novelistic one. Here is where Conrad shows what he approves in both conduct and personality, as well as what he condemns.

(iii)

This argument works just as adequately for the other two novels. *Under Western Eyes* relies considerably for its effect on the deliberate contrast between Razumov and the Professor of Languages. But this does not give us a restatement of the moral outcome or of the human dilemma as it is portrayed in *The Secret Agent*. It provides a closer definition in that both Razumov and the Professor are characterised by a simplicity. As we have seen, the Professor is isolated from the confusions of the world he observes by the moral fairness of the Western world of which he is an integral part, and a symbol. This gives additional weight to his simple moral creed, itself nurtured by his Western views, and explains his simple and sincere relationships with the Haldins, together with his demand that Razumov's should be the same, as when for example he insists that Razumov cannot stay away from the Haldin household any longer. Razumov in his turn shows a degree of simplicity, but this is an aspect of his moral lack of commitment. Conrad shows us through him that the simple way out is a form of self-indulgence and of expedience and therefore provides no answer in the human dilemma. It is only when Razumov gains true moral orientation that he sees the simple answer to all his problems. But once again, the simple answer is not a simple thing to perform. We all know from our own limited experiences how difficult it is to own up. Thus Conrad makes use of common ground we can appreciate when he makes Razumov's confession the climax of his novel, and the point at which his hero achieves moral wholeness. Redemption, as I have already pointed out, is Razumov's having found an existence not founded on falsehood.

The other extension that *Under Western Eyes* makes beyond *The Secret Agent* is in its psychological awareness of the demanding power of love between the sexes. If we attend to the critics, we will be led to believe that Conrad is notoriously bad at dealing with sexual themes, and when writing of love is only assured when dealing with maternal affection, rather than falling in love. *Under Western Eyes* seems to refute much of this—as, to a certain extent, does *Nostromo*. Razumov's moral wholeness comes as a direct result of his falling in love with Nathalie. His morality arises from it. It is the moving force of his redemption, and shows his moral advancement beyond Winnie's state in *The Secret Agent*. The comment in *Under Western Eyes* about the anguish of hearts being extinguished in pure love is not just important as a statement about the cessation of moral doubt. The qualification Conrad puts on the type of love is vital. It must be pure, selfless; like Razumov's, not like Winnie's.

(iv)

This concept of the moral role of love can also be traced without much difficulty through the pages of *Nostromo*. Here we have clearly stated in the relationship between Monygham and Emily Gould, indeed in the charitable outgoing of Emily's whole nature, a claim for the positive relationship between morality and human love. And from this treatment of the most spiritual of all qualities we have a final comment on the achievement of a whole and sound personality in any human being. We have already drawn attention to the fact that in Conrad's moral universe, as in our own, success in terms of the personality is a spiritual thing. The personality is tainted by anything unspiritual, anything, for example, which is merely expedient. There is no salvation in what is material or even just shallow. This is why Nostromo's concept of morality as expedience—any action done by him, or indeed by anyone else, in the hope of reward—only drags one down further into moral complexity and turmoil, loading more and more questions onto the human dilemma. Mitchell's defiance of Sotillo is morally laudable since it is an action on its own, a simple assertion of value opposing an evil force. But it stems from a morality which is limited by its fundamentality and unimaginativeness. Only in the narrowness of its vision does it differ from Emily's out of which comes positive spiritual power.

However, we are once again in danger of losing the proper emphasis. As I have suggested, there is an optimism in these novels, and this, it seems to me, survives largely because Conrad, when he condemns, does so by implication rather than by direct statement. Of course he does damn utterly on occasion. One would be ignoring the meaning of the words if one read Conrad's final description of Ossipon in any other way. But Conrad is anxious to be constructive as well as destructive, and also to show us the anomalies of the shore-bound existence, such as the relativity of strength and weakness in the society of *The Secret Agent*, in such a way as will make a strong appeal to us.

Clearly he shows us the need to integrate our own lives, and the dangers arising out of lack of communication. But deep inside his genius lies a concern for man and his conscience, a worry over loyalties which is, after all, the human dilemma itself. This is the heart of Conrad's appeal to his readers. What he shows is important to us because we too are ultimately a part of this quandary of human activity. Personal reactions to Conrad are strong because, one way or another, we cannot but be involved in what he has to say. And this is the point where the real world and the fictional world merge and become one.

A Short Bibliography

(i)

Joseph Conrad, *Works,* Dent's Collected Edition (London, 1947)

(ii)

Jocelyn Baines, *Joseph Conrad: A Critical Biography* (Weidenfeld & Nicolson, London, 1960)

A. J. Guerard, *Conrad, the Novelist* (Harvard University Press, 1958)

Leo Gurko, *Joseph Conrad, Giant in Exile* (Muller, London, 1962)

Gerard Jean-Aubry, *The Sea Dreamer: A definitive biography of Joseph Conrad* (Allen & Unwin, London, 1957)

F. R. Leavis, *The Great Tradition* (Chatto & Windus, London, 1948)

Edward W. Said, *Joseph Conrad and the Fiction of Autobiography* (Harvard University Press, 1966)

Norman Sherry, *Conrad's Eastern World* (Cambridge University Press, 1966)

R. W. Stallman (ed.), *The Art of Joseph Conrad, A Critical Symposium* (Michigan State University Press, 1960)

J. I. M. Stewart, *Joseph Conrad* (Longmans, London, 1968)

Dorothy Van Ghent, *The English Novel, Form and Function* (Rinehart, New York, 1953)

Index

INDEX

INDEX

INDEX

INDEX

INDEX

INDEX